QUICK LOW-CARB

QUICK LOW-CARB

60 Recipes For A Healthy Fuss-Free Diet

LOSE WEIGHT the safe and easy way with delicious low-carb food that takes less than 30 minutes to cook

EXPERT GUIDANCE provides everything you need to know to start and maintain a low-carbohydrate diet, from breakfasts and soups to meat, poultry and desserts

EACH RECIPE is illustrated step-by-step, with more than 180 stunning photographs to ensure perfect results every time

ELAINE GARDNER

southwater

This edition is published by Southwater, an imprint of Anness Publishing Ltd,
Hermes House, 88–89 Blackfriars Road, London SE1 8HA; tel. 020 7401 2077; fax 020 7633 9499

www.southwaterbooks.com; www.annesspublishing.com

If you like the images in this book and would like to investigate using them for publishing, promotions or advertising, please visit our website www.practicalpictures.com for more information.

UK agent: The Manning Partnership Ltd;
tel. 01225 478444; fax 01225 478440; sales@manning-partnership.co.uk
UK distributor: Grantham Book Services Ltd;
tel. 01476 541080; fax 01476 541061; orders@gbs.tbs-ltd.co.uk
North American agent/distributor: National Book Network;
tel. 301 459 3366; fax 301 429 5746; www.nbnbooks.com
Australian agent/distributor: Pan Macmillan Australia;
tel. 1300 135 113; fax 1300 135 103; customer.service@macmillan.com.au
New Zealand agent/distributor: David Bateman Ltd;
tel. (09) 415 7664; fax (09) 415 8892

Publisher: Joanna Lorenz
Senior Managing Editor: Conor Kilgallon
Editors: Clare Gooden, Lucy Doncaster and Elizabeth Woodland
Production Controller: Wendy Lawson
Designer: Nigel Partridge
Cover Designer: Terry Jeavons
Recipes: Alex Barker, Joanna Farrow, Yasuko Fukuoka, Brian Glover, Nicola Graimes, Becky Johnson, Lucy Knox, Jane Milton, Marlena Spieler
Photography: Nicki Dowey, Amanda Heywood, William Lingwood, Thomas Odulate, Craig Robertson, Simon Smith

ETHICAL TRADING POLICY
Because of our ongoing ecological investment programme, you, as our customer, can have the pleasure and reassurance of knowing that a tree is being cultivated on your behalf to naturally replace the materials used to make the book you are holding. For further information about this scheme, go to www.annesspublishing.com/trees

Previously published as part of a larger volume, *The Low-Carbohydrate Cookbook*

NOTES

Bracketed terms are intended for American readers.
For all recipes, quantities are given in both metric and imperial measures and, where appropriate, in standard cups and spoons. Follow one set of measures, but not a mixture, because they are not interchangeable.
Standard spoon and cup measures are level. 1 tsp = 5ml, 1 tbsp = 15ml, 1 cup = 250ml/8fl oz.
Australian standard tablespoons are 20ml. Australian readers should use 3 tsp in place of 1 tbsp for measuring small quantities.
American pints are 16fl oz/2 cups. American readers should use 20fl oz/2.5 cups in place of 1 pint when measuring liquids.
Electric oven temperatures in this book are for conventional ovens. When using a fan oven, the temperature will probably need to be reduced by about 10–20°C/20–40°F. Since ovens vary, you should check with your manufacturer's instruction book for guidance.
The nutritional analysis given for each recipe is calculated per portion (i.e. serving or item), unless otherwise stated. If the recipe gives a range, such as Serves 4–6, then the nutritional analysis will be for the smaller portion size, i.e. 6 servings. Measurements for sodium do not include salt added to taste.
Medium (US large) eggs are used unless otherwise stated.

Main front cover image shows Scallops with Fennel and Bacon – for recipe, see page 74

Contents

introduction

A LOW-CARBOHYDRATE DIET is a healthy way of eating, and a good option for achieving rapid, effective weight loss. By making a few simple changes to your lifestyle, incorporating exercise into your routine, and adjusting your eating habits, it can become a successful long-term weight maintenance programme.

Millions of people around the world are adopting a low-carbohydrate diet as a way of losing weight, lowering cholesterol and improving overall health. It is an effective and satisfying diet, on which you can eat a wide variety of delicious foods. A low-carbohydrate diet can be used to tackle weight gain or simply incorporated into your lifestyle as a healthy way of maintaining your ideal weight.

Social, economic and cultural changes, which affect us all, mean that the rate of obesity is increasing, and there is an obsession with weight loss in the Western world. However, improving a person's overall health profile is equally important. A lower carbohydrate, high-protein diet with a healthy proportion of the right types of fat provides a healthier way of eating long-term, combined with weight loss.

It is important to contact your doctor before changing eating patterns or starting any weight loss regime, especially if you suffer from diabetes, high blood pressure or a kidney disorder. A low-carbohydrate diet is not recommended for children, the elderly or pregnant women.

SCIENCE MADE SIMPLE

To lose weight, a very simple formula applies: energy intake must be controlled and output increased in the form of activity. The part of weight management that is often open to debate concerns the amount and ideal proportions of macronutrients (such as carbohydrates, protein and fats) that should be consumed in the diet.

Traditionally, increasing carbohydrate foods was encouraged to add bulk and satisfy hunger; however, the effect of carbohydrates on blood fat levels and insulin response is now better understood, and a lower carbohydrate intake is recommended by many nutritionists. A lower carbohydrate, high protein, healthy fat diet is just as good as other energy controlling diets in reducing weight. The difference is that this diet is more effective in improving body composition: in other words, it enhances the loss of fat while retaining the muscle that is often reduced when losing weight.

Left: *For successful weight loss and long-term weight maintenance, a healthy diet is essential. This may involve changing your lifestyle and adopting new eating habits.*

Above: *A healthy low-carb diet includes plenty of fresh fish, meat and vegetables, along with essential dairy products.*

A PRACTICAL APPROACH

Too often, diet advice encourages diving into a new way of eating without serious thought or sufficient preparation. It is no wonder that it is difficult to continue with some diets when essential ingredients are missing from regular shopping lists or cupboards are full of foods that should be avoided. This book provides all of the information you need to start and maintain a new eating pattern. As well as explaining in clear and simple terms how the diet actually works, it provides details on getting started, with practical suggestions for implementing the diet, selecting low-carbohydrate snacks, and coping with everyday events, such as eating out at restaurants. These sit alongside great ideas for menu planning and delicious recipes to help make this eating plan really special.

Additionally, the book tackles modern issues in a down-to-earth manner, including vegetarianism and health tips, with an update on newer food items, such as probiotic drinks and yogurt bio-cultures. An extensive guide to ingredients provides background information on the foods you can enjoy and those you should avoid. Step-by-step pictures demonstrate easy and healthy ways of preparing different ingredients to encourage confident cooking. Essential kitchen utensils are examined alongside the top ten healthy cooking methods and quick, simple ideas for using the microwave.

Anyone who has been on a diet before will agree that the most difficult part of weight management is keeping the weight off. Long-term weight maintenance is discussed with suggestions on modifying daily eating patterns, taking account of the need to fit holidays and special occasions into your new lifestyle.

Below: *Leading an active life will enable you to maintain your ideal weight.*

the low-carb approach

ON A LOW-CARBOHYDRATE diet, body composition is improved as the body loses more fat and preserves lean muscle tissue, which would otherwise be lost. Whenever you do any exercise – something that is always recommended on a diet – you will add lean muscle while still losing fat.

By following a diet regime based on lower levels of carbohydrate with a higher protein content, a higher proportion of body fat is lost. This means that more muscle, or lean body mass, is preserved. In turn, this gives the body improved definition and shape, especially if it is toned up through regular exercise. Performing exercise will also help to maintain strength in the muscles.

COMPARATIVE SATIETY OF FOOD

Hunger pangs are often a problem when dieting. High-protein foods make you feel full so they suppress appetite and subsequent energy intake. Even when different types of foods that contain the same number of calories are eaten, those higher in protein are more filling than those containing either carbohydrate or fat, so you should feel less hungry on a high-protein diet.

THE EFFECT ON BONES

There are several ways of maintaining strong bones, and adopting a good diet and taking regular exercise helps to keep bone strength as high as possible. A healthy diet, including plenty of calcium-rich foods, such as milk, yogurt and nuts, and adequate amounts of vitamin D (found in oily fish), is extremely important. After the age of 35, calcium is gradually lost from bones as part of the natural ageing process, so the intake of calcium-rich foods should increase. In women, the loss occurs at a much faster rate after the menopause because of the loss of the protective effects of the female hormone oestrogen.

Below: *High-protein foods make you feel full, meaning there is less chance of giving in to temptation and ruining the diet.*

THE EFFECT ON THE KIDNEYS

For many years now there has been some controversy surrounding whether high protein intake causes damage to the kidneys. Intakes of up to 2.2g protein per kg body weight per day do not appear to have any adverse effect on kidney function. For someone weighing 100kg/220lb, this is the equivalent of eating seven 200g/7oz (130g/4½oz drained weight) cans of tuna a day.

BLOOD FATS

Blood cholesterol

An excess of cholesterol in the blood increases the risk of heart disease. Foods high in saturated fats increase blood cholesterol levels. Foods that contain cholesterol have little effect on blood cholesterol levels. This is because there are two types of cholesterol.

- LDL (low-density lipoprotein) cholesterol can slowly build up in the arteries and cause a heart attack.
- HDL (high-density lipoprotein) cholesterol, sometimes known as "good" cholesterol, carries cholesterol back to the liver, thus lowering the risk of a heart attack.

Blood triglycerides

These are fats that can be made in the body or absorbed from food. Diets that are high in carbohydrates, especially refined carbohydrates such as white rice, bread and pasta, and alcohol, can increase blood triglycerides. People with high levels of blood triglycerides have an increased risk of heart disease, and are more likely to be overweight or have diabetes.

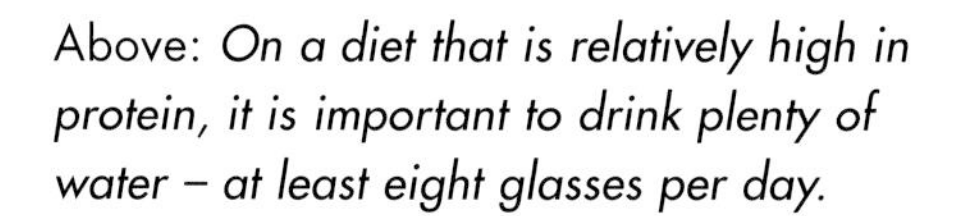

Above: *On a diet that is relatively high in protein, it is important to drink plenty of water – at least eight glasses per day.*

Not cutting down on the amount of protein eaten and choosing food sources wisely provides the benefits that aid weight loss with good health and no risk of kidney damage. However, it is important to remember that the body needs more fluid to break down protein than fat or carbohydrate, so drink at least eight glasses of water per day.

THE EFFECT ON BLOOD SUGAR

When carbohydrate foods are eaten a hormone called insulin is secreted into the bloodstream. This signals the body to remove excess sugar from the bloodstream and store it for future use. When excess insulin is produced this results in a low level of blood sugar, with unpleasant symptoms such as dizziness, tiredness, low energy levels and food cravings. Research has shown that a diet higher in protein produces a lower insulin response. This reduces swings in blood sugar levels and stabilizes them between meals.

Foods such as peas, beans, lentils, fruits and vegetables contain carbohydrate alongside protein, vitamins and minerals. These often contain slowly absorbed carbohydrates, which do not cause large swings in blood sugar, together with essential fibre and valuable antioxidants.

Above: *To ensure your bones stay strong, incorporate regular exercise, such as cycling, into your new healthy lifestyle.*

THE EFFECT ON BLOOD FATS

Eating a diet that is low in carbohydrates, especially avoiding those from simple, refined sources, means that blood triglyceride concentrations can be significantly reduced. For protein sources, eat lean meat, lower fat dairy products, white and oily fish, along with nuts, peas, beans, lentils and soya products. Eating these foods can help to lower blood cholesterol levels. A diet that is low in carbohydrate, high in protein, and contains healthy fats, can be extremely beneficial to health and can help achieve weight loss.

HOMOCYSTEINE

Homocysteine is a compound made in the body and normally found in low levels in the blood. A higher level of homocysteine is one of several factors that may play a role in damaging the lining of blood vessels, linking it to heart disease. The three vitamins folate, B_6 (found in fruit and vegetables) and B_{12} (the main source in the diet is meat) act to lower homocysteine levels. Eating a diet rich in fruit, vegetables and meat may be a way of minimizing the homocysteine levels in the blood.

Below: *Complex carbohydrates, such as wholemeal (whole-wheat) grains, pasta and beans, provide slow-release energy.*

different types of carbohydrate

THE KEY TO success on a low-carbohydrate diet is not simply cutting out all forms of carbohydrate. Instead, recognize the different types of carbohydrate available and understand which must be avoided completely, which are fine to eat occasionally and which are good, healthy sources of carbohydrate.

Carbohydrates are found in a variety of foods, and they provide energy. Some foods supply additional nutrients, such as valuable vitamins or minerals, or they may provide carbohydrate in a slow-release form that sustains energy levels over a period of time and avoids large swings in blood sugar levels. To promote weight loss, energy intake needs to be kept in check and only the best types of carbohydrates eaten.

FRUITS AND VEGETABLES

Natural sugars can be found in fruits, and these are balanced with healthy amounts of fibre and valuable supplies of vitamins, minerals and antioxidants. Non-starchy vegetables, such as broccoli, cauliflower, mushrooms, spinach and cabbage, contain slowly absorbed complex carbohydrates alongside other beneficial nutrients. These can be eaten freely.

Pure fruit and vegetable juices concentrate the complex carbohydrates and natural sugars, so their intake should be limited to one serving per day.

Starchy fruit and vegetables, such as potatoes, bananas and yams, contain large amounts of quickly absorbed carbohydrates and should be avoided.

PEAS, BEANS AND LENTILS

The slow-release carbohydrates found in peas and beans, such as chickpeas or red kidney beans, provide sustained energy. They are also good sources of low-fat proteins, fibre and the essential B vitamins, folic acid and iron. These should be eaten regularly.

Below: *Peas, beans and lentils should be a major part of your low-carbohydrate diet. Try adding them to salads or casseroles.*

Above: *A valuable source of fibre and vitamins and minerals, a portion of fruit makes an ideal mid-morning snack.*

GRAINS AND CEREALS

All types of grain and cereal contain a considerable amount of carbohydrate. If necessary, small amounts of these wholegrain products can be eaten. Foods such as barley, millet and oats (which are proportionately higher in protein) are recommended.

REFINED CARBOHYDRATES

These are foods that contain refined sugars and flours, such as cakes, biscuits (cookies), sugars, fruit squashes, white bread, white rice or pasta. These foods should all be eliminated from the diet as they contain large amounts of quickly absorbed carbohydrate.

Carbohydrates are also hidden in many processed foods, such as ketchup, sauces, pickles, canned and packet soups, and desserts, and these should be avoided.

GLYCAEMIC INDEX

The glycaemic index (GI) is a measure of how quickly a food raises blood sugar levels in the body. It ranks foods from 0 to 100.

Foods with a high glycaemic index are digested quickly and so cause a rapid flow of blood sugar into the bloodstream. This in turn stimulates the body to produce a large rush of insulin to control the blood sugar.

Foods with a low glycaemic index release glucose more gradually and to a lesser degree, thereby avoiding the large swings in blood sugar levels due to high levels of insulin production. These are the foods to select. Low GI foods also help to satisfy appetite, which is a bonus when trying to lose weight.

FIVE A DAY

Evidence shows that people who eat more fruit and vegetables reduce their risk of coronary heart disease, some cancers and gut problems. As a group of foods, fruit and vegetables are low in fat and energy, and a good source of fibre.

Below: *Refined carbohydrates with few nutrients, such as white bread, pasta and sugar, should be avoided.*

GLYCAEMIC INDEX MEASURE OF SOME COMMON FOODS

Food	Glycaemic Index (GI)
White rice, cooked	87
Baked potato	85
Wholemeal (whole-wheat) bread	71
White bread	70
Baked beans	48
Apple	38
Cooked lentils	30
Peanuts	14

They are also rich in potassium, low in salt, and provide a range of vitamins and antioxidants, which are important for health.

Fruit and vegetables also contain anti-carcinogens called phytochemicals. These neutralize the effects of substances that may promote cancer. Brassicas (such as cabbage and broccoli) are thought to be rich in one such compound called glucosinolates. Other important phytochemicals include lycopene, found in tomatoes, and allium, found in garlic, onions and leeks.

Five portions or 400g/14oz of fruit and vegetables per day is the minimum required to promote health. These five portions will provide minimal energy, and the carbohydrates they contain are balanced by extra nutrients. Only one portion per day should be fruit or vegetable juice. Each of the following counts as one portion:

- 1 piece of fruit (apple, orange or peach)
- 2 small fruits (plums, kiwis, satsumas)
- 1 large slice of melon or pineapple
- 1 cupful of berries
- 2–3 tablespoons stewed or canned fruit
- 1 glass (150ml/¼ pint/⅔ cup) fruit or vegetable juice
- 2 tablespoons raw, cooked, frozen or canned vegetables
- 1 dessert bowl full of salad

Fruit and vegetables should be eaten as fresh as possible. Vegetables should be lightly boiled, steamed or cooked in the microwave to retain their goodness.

Above: *Some fruits and vegetables are very high in carbohydrate so they should be avoided on a low-carb diet plan – these include potatoes, yams and plantains.*

FOODS TO AVOID

Foods that contain high amounts of carbohydrate:

- Bread, cakes and biscuits (cookies)
- Pasta and noodles
- Rice, maize, buckwheat, bulgur wheat and rye
- Starchy fruits and vegetables (banana, yam, potato, sweet potato)
- Cereals, including most refined breakfast cereals

Foods that contain refined sugars:

- Brown and white sugar and honey
- Sweets (candies)
- Fruit squashes and carbonated, sweetened drinks
- Jam (jelly), marmalade, syrup and treacle (molasses)
- Ketchups, pickles and chutneys
- Ice cream

Foods that contain refined starches:

- Canned and packet soups
- Bought custards and desserts
- Ready-made sauces
- Stock (bouillon) granules and cubes

good fats and bad fats

MOST TRADITIONAL diet programmes advise avoiding all fats. However, there are many healthy fats that the body needs to function properly. A low-carbohydrate diet recommends eating these "good" fats to help stabilize cholesterol levels, protect your heart and boost general health.

The fats in food are concentrated sources of energy. On a weight management programme it is essential to limit the amount of fat consumed to keep calorie intake down. However, some fats are essential for health, and including the right type of fat is just as important as reducing the amount of fat.

Omega-3s are the healthy fats to look for. These fats reduce the stickiness of the blood so blood clots are less likely to block arteries. They also reduce the level of triglycerides in the blood, which are a major risk factor for heart disease. Finally, omega-3 fats help the heart to beat regularly. In summary, omega-3s are the fats to choose for a healthy heart.

DANGER: AVOID THESE FATS

Foods that contain saturated fat and trans fats raise blood cholesterol levels, which are a major risk factor in the development of heart disease. These foods must be avoided.

Saturated fats are found in:

- Fatty meats
- High-fat sausages
- Crisps (US potato chips)
- Pies and pastries
- Lard (white cooking fat) and butter
- Double (heavy) cream
- Chocolate

Trans fats are found in:

- Hard margarines
- Fatty fast foods
- Pre-prepared meals
- Biscuits (cookies)
- Cakes

Above: *Avoid prepared salad dressings as these are often high in fat. Use olive oil and fresh lemon juice to add flavour.*

Above: *Choose fresh tuna instead of canned, wherever possible, as the canned variety has lost its good omega-3 fats.*

SOURCES OF OMEGA-3 FATS

The main source of omega-3 fats is oily fish, such as kippers, herring, mackerel, pilchards, salmon and sardines. Fresh tuna is also an excellent source of healthy fats, but when tuna is canned it loses its good omega-3s. (This does not happen with other canned fish so they remain a great choice.) Try to eat fish at least twice a week as part of your low-carbohydrate diet.

HOW MUCH FAT TO EAT

One key factor to weight reduction is limiting the amount of fat eaten to under a third of energy intake. On a diet that consists of a 3.5 megajoule/1500 calorie a day total intake, daily fat consumption of around 50g/2oz is recommended.

This fat intake should come predominantly from the healthy heart types of food with small additional amounts from olive oil, seeds (such as sesame, pumpkin and sunflower) and avocados. Those who do not like oily fish or are vegetarian can take omega-3 fats in the form of a supplement. Pure varieties are available containing 0.5–1g omega-3 fats in the form of EPA (eicosapentaenoic acid) and DHA (docosahexaenoic acid) in a daily capsule or liquid form.

FAT AND WEIGHT LOSS

All of the healthy heart fats that you should be eating can easily slot into a diet that provides the dual benefits of working towards weight loss and good heart health.

Oily fish, nuts, enriched eggs and soya, all of which contain these healthy fats, are also good sources of protein and an excellent base for a low-carbohydrate diet. Regularly including these foods rather than building your menu around meat helps to keep your intake of saturated fat down. It is recommended that you eat one or two portions of oily fish per week in addition to other white fish and seafood.

sources of protein

A HEALTHY DIET must include protein, and when you are cutting back on carbohydrate foods, protein becomes even more important. However, if you increase your intake of protein, be sure to drink plenty of water, as the body needs more fluid to break down protein than carbohydrate or fat.

Protein is an essential part of the diet. The cells of the body must be replaced constantly, and protein is the only nutrient that can build, maintain and repair our cells. It is also needed for the structure of bones, muscle and skin, and for chemicals such as hormones and enzymes in the body. The antibodies that fight illness and infection, and haemoglobin, which transports oxygen around the body, are also proteins.

There are two main sources of protein. Animal sources are meat, poultry, fish and shellfish, eggs, milk, cheese and yogurt. Vegetable sources are peas, beans and lentils, nuts, seeds and meat substitutes, such as mycoproteins (Quorn), soya and textured vegetable protein.

The quality of a protein depends upon its composition and whether it is able to supply the building blocks that the body needs. As a general rule, proteins from animal or fish sources supply all of these building blocks in one food. Vegetable sources have to be combined or eaten together on the same day to provide them all. This is not usually a problem as foods are commonly eaten in combinations. The exception is soya and its products, such as tofu, as it has similar protein quality to animal protein; this is an excellent choice of food.

PROCESSED FOODS

Many processed foods, such as meat or fish pies, burgers, pastries, grill steaks and sausages, contain a large amount of carbohydrate in addition to protein. Bread, rusk and other carbohydrates are often added to these products to bulk them out. Additionally, many of these products are high in saturated fat and do not contribute to a diet for a healthy heart.

It is important to avoid foods that are coated with crumbs or batter, including chicken or fish products, as these are loaded with quickly absorbed carbohydrate. Sauces in ready-made dishes, for example casseroles or curries, can also be a problem as many are thickened with sugars, for example sweet and sour sauce, or pure starch. Overall, it is important to avoid processed sources of protein.

QUANTITY OF PROTEIN TO EAT

Protein is not stored in the body, so any extra protein is broken down and used as a source of energy. Protein foods can help reduce the feeling of hunger more than other energy-providing foods, so they are vital for a successful low-carbohydrate diet.

As well as encouraging weight loss, eating lower fat protein foods or those containing healthy fats, can improve your blood fats profile. Aim to include two large helpings of protein foods, plus milk and yogurt, per day.

Below: *Fish sources of protein provide our bodies with the building blocks we need to maintain healthy cells.*

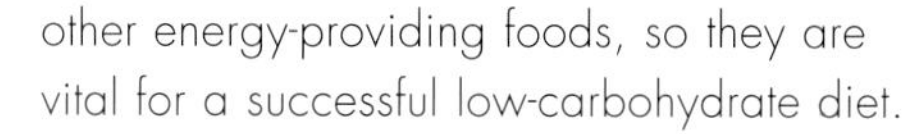

VEGETARIAN OPTIONS

This programme is suitable for vegetarians as well as those who eat meat. The recommendations of what to eat and what to exclude differ slightly, but it is simply a matter of selecting wisely from the choices available (listed below). The energy requirements for vegetarians are exactly the same as for meat-eaters.

Protein:

- Semi-skimmed (low-fat) milk
- Yogurt
- Eggs
- Cheeses made without rennet
- Nuts, seeds and pulses
- Soya and its products (milk, tofu, miso, tahini, tempeh, textured vegetable protein)
- Mycoproteins (Quorn)

Fats:

- Olive oil,
- Rapeseed (canola) oil and spread
- Nuts and seeds

Carbohydrates:

- Fruit
- Vegetables
- Pure fruit and vegetable juices
- Peas, beans and lentils

assessing your weight

BEING OVERWEIGHT is not only psychologically demoralizing, it is also unhealthy and can lead to serious medical problems. There is no quick solution – losing weight takes time and commitment. Closely monitor how your diet progresses, but do not let yourself become obsessed with the figures.

Being overweight impinges on many aspects of daily life and makes them less enjoyable. Excess weight can also lead to a poorer quality of life with a shorter life span. Obese people are two to three times more likely to die prematurely than those who are leaner and, on average, being obese reduces life span by nine years. There are several simple ways of measuring your weight and checking that you are a healthy weight for your size.

BODY MASS INDEX

A common way of measuring whether an individual is overweight is to record the body mass index (BMI). This is based on your height and weight and can easily be worked out using the simple chart below. Measure height and weight without wearing shoes, draw a line across from the height and up from the weight – the point at which the lines meet shows the BMI category that you fall into.

Another way of working out BMI is by dividing your weight in kilograms by your height in metres squared:

$$\frac{\text{Weight (kg)}}{\text{Height (m)}^2}$$

Body mass index (BMI) is a useful guide for assessing health risk.

- BMI of less than 19 indicates that the person is underweight and may need to put on weight.
- BMI between 19 and 25 indicates a healthy weight, and this is the range in which to stay.
- A BMI of 26 to 30 indicates that the person is overweight. Weight should not rise any further; the person should try and reduce their weight.
- A BMI of over 30 means that health is at risk and the person is classified as obese. It indicates that it is time to lose weight and become more active.

PERCENTAGE BODY FAT

This is often calculated in health clubs or gyms by bio-electrical impedance analysis (BIA). A small current of electricity is passed between electrodes placed on the hands and feet. The amount of lean body tissue is worked out from the drop in voltage caused by the resistance of the body. The amount of fat can then be calculated.

In a normal-weight, healthy adult the amount of body fat varies from 10–25 per cent in males and from 15–35 per cent in females. In cases of obesity, fat can be as high as 60–70 per cent of body weight.

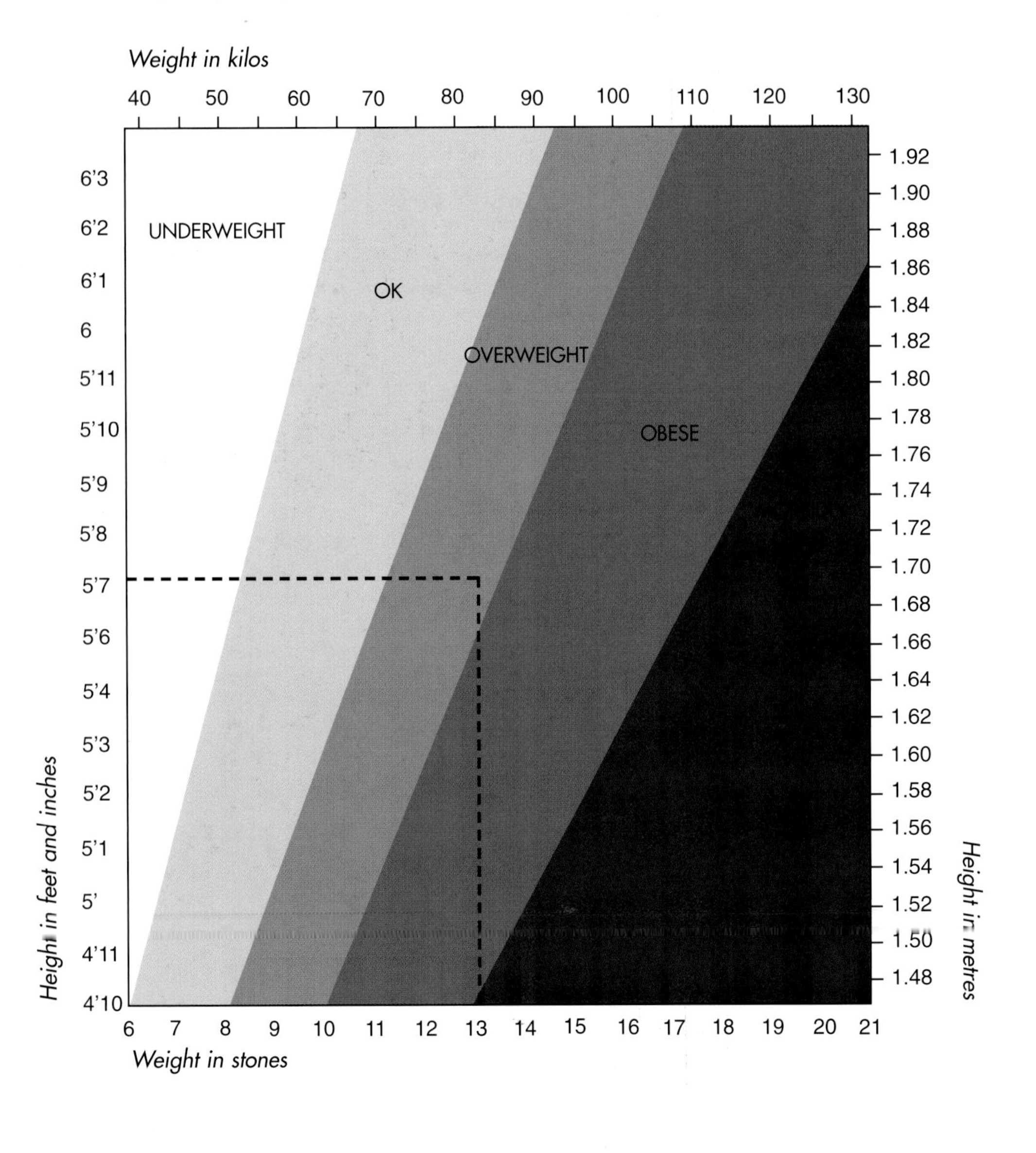

Left: *Use this chart to calculate your body mass index (BMI) and decide whether you are a healthy weight.*

CLOTHES

Often, it is not complicated measurements but clothes that tell the true story. Realizing that tight clothes are becoming more comfortable is a marvellous indicator to boost enthusiasm for maintaining weight loss. The pleasure of being able to go down a size in clothes can be one of the greatest incentives to continue with a healthy weight-loss programme.

WEIGHT-LOSS AIMS

An ideal weight loss is between 0.5–1kg/1–2lb per week. This may not seem very much, but the loss needs to be consistent. Over six months this level of weekly weight loss will result in a reduction of over 22kg/49lb, or 3½ stone. Even with a weight loss of just 5–10kg/11–22lb or 1½ stone there can be a noticeable improvement in back and joint pain, and a reduction in breathlessness. A loss of just 5–10 per cent of body weight can reduce blood pressure, lower the risk of angina and improve your blood cholesterol levels.

Left: *On a low-carb programme, avoid toast at breakfast and try low-fat natural yogurt with added fresh fruit instead.*

Below: *Weigh youself once a week and record your weight on a chart – you will soon see a downward trend emerging.*

ARE YOU AN APPLE OR A PEAR?

People who carry too much weight around their waist have an increased risk of developing heart disease or diabetes. This body shape is commonly known as an "apple shape". Those who carry excess weight around their hips are "pear shaped", which is less harmful to health.

	WAIST MEASUREMENT	
	At risk	High risk
MEN	94cm/37in	102cm/40in
WOMEN	80cm/32in	88cm/35in

SCALES

This is probably the easiest and most common way of measuring weight. Weight should be checked under the same conditions each time – ideally, without wearing shoes, in minimal clothing, at the same time of day and using the same set of scales. Weight fluctuates on a daily basis, so it is important not to get obsessed with the exact readings. Instead, use them as a longer-term indication of progress when losing weight. It may be useful to draw a simple chart on which you can note your weight once per week. Over a period of time the downward trend will gradually begin to show and you will feel proud of your achievement.

how to start a diet

THE HARDEST PART of adopting a new healthy eating lifestyle or embarking on a weight-loss programme is finding the motivation to get started. There is a lot more involved than many people realize, including clearing out cupboards, buying in the basic ingredients and equipment, and drawing up firm eating plans.

Starting a weight-loss programme or diet may sound easy, but if you rush into it without proper consideration and preparation, there is a real danger that you may not achieve your goals. Preparation, both mental and practical, gives a greater chance of succeeding.

THE STAGES OF CHANGE

The first step in getting started is to decide on your readiness for change. This can be represented by "The Stages of Change".

There are five recognized stages in this model, which everybody needs to progress through: pre-contemplation, contemplation, preparation, action and maintenance. Pre-contemplation is when someone is not actively thinking about weight loss but is aware of the need to do so. Contemplation is when there is active thought about the need to lose weight. Preparation refers to getting ready for weight loss, which includes researching the programme. Action is making the decision to lose weight and beginning to implement the starting regime. Maintenance is having the motivation to keep the weight-loss programme going and deciding to continue positively until all of the goals are achieved. Track your progress through these stages.

Below: *Prepare vegetables and keep them in the refrigerator or take them to work so you always have a supply of healthy snacks.*

MOTIVATION

A person's expressed degree of readiness to change is described as their motivation. When starting a diet, it is important to focus on the positive and think about how much slimmer you want to be rather than how fat you are. As a positive incentive, list the reasons for losing weight and all of those things that will be possible when the excess weight has gone.

A useful way to check your readiness for change is to draw a straight line. Label one end "not ready" and the other "ready". In the middle put "unsure". Honestly mark on this line the point you are at. If you are not ready, then it is important to explore why there is this feeling of reluctance. Address any problems before starting the weight-loss programme as it is imperative to remove any barriers or obstacles in your way.

BARRIERS TO CHANGE

Everybody will face barriers to changing their eating habits, and addressing these barriers makes it easier to achieve goals. It is not possible to control and change all barriers and this should be acknowledged.

A common barrier to change is the amount of money available for food. The cost of the diet needs to be compared to the money spent on poorer quality foods, including sweets (candies), chocolates, cookies and processed foods. The price of food in local shops and access to cheaper out-of-town supermarkets should also be considered. The ability to prepare suitable foods, facilities and time available are important factors. Many foods, such as salad leaves, cold meats, canned fish and nuts require little time to prepare or cook; they simply have to be added to the shopping list to replace prepared foods.

GETTING READY: THE CHECKLIST

Deal with the following before starting:

- Assess your readiness for change by listing reasons for losing weight and the things you cannot do due to your excess weight.
- Set realistic targets to help achieve your goals.
- Consider any barriers to change and remove as many as possible.
- Keep a food and feelings chart.
- Clear your kitchen cupboards of unwanted items.
- Check for any useful equipment, such as a blender and steamer, to ensure they are readily accessible.
- Draw up eating plans and shopping lists.
- Ensure basic food items, such as fresh herbs and rapeseed (canola) oil, are purchased.
- Prepare food in advance and freeze it if this helps.
- Practise saying "no" aloud to reject some foods.
- Identify someone to whom you can talk if necessary.
- Set a date to start.

Lifestyle barriers and situations that tempt a break in diet need to be acknowledged and avoided. If eating out plays a significant role in your life, choosing appropriately from a menu is important. Keeping alcohol consumption under control is also integral to long-term success. Although there will be times when you slip up, special occasions should not be seen as an excuse for breaking the diet. Instead, they should be incorporated into the regime.

Unhappiness, loneliness, boredom or jealousy are all feelings that can propel people into eating more. Emotions should be recognized for what they are to avoid seeking comfort in food. Charting feelings and food can help identify comfort eating. For example, writing down on a daily basis the time, place, company and activity alongside the food eaten can help. Note how you felt before eating – if you were hungry – and how you felt after eating. This can provide clues to genuine hunger and times when eating is a response to other influences. By seeking support from family and friends, and thinking about coping strategies, more control can be gained.

Above: *One of the biggest challenges to your will-power will occur at parties and when eating out with friends or family – try to plan ahead for these situations.*

Below: *Snacks like unsalted nuts need absolutely no preparation, so they are ideal to keep on stand-by, whether at work or at home, in case of hunger pangs.*

SETTING GOALS

There are three main areas to think about when deciding to change – importance, confidence and readiness. Importance is to do with "why?", "is it worthwhile?", "what will change?", and "do I really want to?". Confidence deals with areas such as "how will I do it?" and "will I succeed ?". Low levels of confidence can also affect a person's feelings and thoughts about the importance of change. Both of these affect the readiness to change – the "when" question, with thoughts such as "should I do it now?".

Goal setting is an excellent way to approach the challenge of weight loss. It is similar to planning a long journey in small stages to reduce the overall task into more manageable chunks. The ultimate goal of losing weight can be divided into strategies on how to succeed. For this regime the strategies include eating only healthy fats in the right quantities, taking more exercise, limiting the consumption of unhealthy, refined carbohydrates and eating large portions of lower-fat protein foods.

These strategies can then be divided into specific targets. Taking a target of eating only healthy fats in the right quantities as an example, ways to achieve this can include eating oily fish twice per week, using rapeseed (canola) oil in cooking, and eating nuts as the basis for a main meal once per week.

Drawing up a list of clearly achievable targets is one way of remaining positive and confident throughout the programme. This makes the ultimate goal easier to grasp. Learn to be in charge of eating by saying "no" with conviction and being assertive about what you do eat.

the importance of exercise

WHEN TRYING to lose weight, it is important that you exercise as well as controlling your diet. Any exercise is better than none, so do whatever you can, whenever you can. The best way of sticking to a new exercise programme, however, is to make the exercise part of your daily routine.

Exercise is good for you, and it is more important than usual when trying to lose weight. Weight is based on energy balance. If more calories (or energy) are consumed than burned up, there is weight gain; if more energy is used up than is actually eaten, this will help weight loss.

HEALTH BENEFITS FOR ALL

Regular exercise has been shown to reduce depression and stress, regulate appetite, boost self-confidence, and improve sleep quality. Other conditions that can be improved by regular exercise include heart disease, diabetes and osteoporosis.

Exercise helps in the prevention and treatment of heart disease and strokes by controlling important risk factors such as high blood pressure and high blood cholesterol. In diabetes, regular activity improves the body's sensitivity to insulin and reduces the risk of developing type 2 (late onset) diabetes. Regular exercise also strengthens bones and prevents osteoporosis. Weight-bearing exercise such as running, jogging, climbing stairs, skipping or aerobics is especially beneficial.

THE BEST EXERCISE

To the question of which exercise is best, the answer is "any exercise that you like". Anything that gets the heart pumping is good.

Walking is the most important weight-loss activity. The pace should be faster than normal but without over-exertion. Walking aids weight loss because it is weight bearing, uses the large muscle groups, makes the body breathe more frequently and deeply, and increases heart rate.

Regular aerobic activity, such as swimming, cycling, dancing, skipping, running, rowing or aerobics, can result in a big energy deficit in the body.

Above: *Even pleasurable activities like gardening use up more energy than remaining sedentary, so count as exercise.*

THE AMOUNT OF EXERCISE

It is recommended that everyone takes at least 30 minutes daily exercise on an average of five days per week. For those trying to lose weight this should be increased to 60 minutes per day, five days per week. However, it is important to remember that any exercise is better than none. It may take a few weeks to build up to 60 minutes per day so do not lose heart.

To help include all these different types of activity, it is a good idea to have different slots (in its broadest sense) for exercise throughout the day rather than limiting it to once a day at a particular time. It is also a good idea to aim for regular aerobic activity and at least one walk of over 30 minutes per day.

LOSING FAT NOT MUSCLE

Wanting to lose weight means wanting to lose fat from your body, not muscle. Recent studies have shown that weight loss diets containing moderate amounts of carbohydrate and higher proportions of protein improve the use of body fat as an energy source while maintaining more muscle. The result is that your body shape will change over time. It is not yet fully understood how this works, but it is thought to be due to an effect on hormone levels.

BODY IMAGE

Health is often not the main reason that people want to lose weight. The majority want to shed pounds to improve their overall body image. Using exercise as part of a plan to improve body image is excellent as it helps to tone up muscles and improve appearance.

EXERCISE IDEAS

Household chores and normal routines make a valuable contribution to the exercise quota. The following activities can be incorporated into daily life:

- Using the stairs instead of the lift
- Walking rather than taking the bus or car
- Walking one bus stop further away than usual
- Dancing
- Gardening
- Housework, such as window cleaning or shopping
- Playing with the children
- Walking the dog
- Do-it-yourself (DIY)
- Hiding the TV remote control

getting support while losing weight

ACHIEVING SUCCESS on your new weight-loss programme is only possible if all barriers to change are overcome. Gaining the support of family and friends is crucial, and by allowing time for preparing food and enjoying breakfast, for example, eating habits will be vastly improved.

Keeping the key points in focus is important in order to lose weight. The mental and physical preparation has been explained, along with the need for a firm commitment, but the area that is too often forgotten is the need to acknowledge and remove all obstacles that may hamper progress.

Losing weight is about energy balance – the amount of energy consumed needs to be lower than the amount of energy burnt up by living plus exercise. For example, 450g/1lb fat contains 3,500 calories, so to lose 450g/1lb per week, there needs to be a calorie deficit between intake and expenditure of 500 calories per day. To increase energy output, at least 60 minutes of activity is required five days a week.

It is important to remember the health messages when losing weight to reduce the risk of illnesses such as heart disease, type 2 diabetes, cancer and osteoporosis. The choice of food must be taken into consideration. Carbohydrate intake should be reduced to cut back on energy intake and food groups selected wisely to keep blood sugar levels in check. The diet should include five portions of fruit and vegetables per day (from non-starchy sources), a regular intake of peas, beans and lentils, and small amounts of wholegrain cereals or those grains that contain a higher proportion of fats and protein to carbohydrate. Refined carbohydrates, including those hidden in processed foods, should be avoided.

Above: *Snacks like unsalted nuts need absolutely no preparation, so they are ideal to keep on stand-by, whether at work or at home, in case of hunger pangs.*

Left: *Quick and nutritious fruit smoothies or freshly squeezed fruit juices make a filling and nutritious treat at any time of day.*

Fats should be limited as they are concentrated sources of energy. Using lean meat, nuts, seeds, soya and skimmed-milk products reduces fat intake considerably. Including two portions of oily fish per week alongside white fish and shellfish also keeps the fat intake under control and ensures the diet includes a healthier type of fat.

Protein choices should exclude processed foods that contain large amounts of carbohydrates and saturated fats. Two large helpings of lean meat, poultry, fish, eggs, nuts, peas, beans and lentils, soya or mycoprotein (such as Quorn) daily are ideal along with regular consumption of skimmed milk and low-fat yogurt.

EATING PATTERNS

People who eat regular meals find it easier to control their weight. This enables the body to keep blood sugar levels more stable, and there is comfort in knowing when the next meal will happen. This way true feelings of hunger and fullness are more easily recognized by the body, which helps to keep binge eating under control.

Breakfast is a must in a regular pattern, and recent studies have shown that those who skip breakfast are 450 per cent more likely to be obese.

Snacking between meals does not in itself encourage weight gain – in fact, those who enjoy at least one snack per day alongside regular meals are less likely to become obese. It is the additional energy that is consumed through poor snack choices and bigger portions that is often to blame. Low-energy, high-nutrient foods, such as fruit, nuts or seeds, are ideal for snacks.

INCLUDE THE FAMILY

Everyone needs support and this may come from family, friends and even work colleagues. It is especially important to involve those in your household as any change in eating habits may affect them. Communication is vital for success, and you have to voice the negative feelings about being overweight, making it clear to everyone why weight loss is so important.

Children must not be put on any weight reducing regime unless they are under the direct supervision of a doctor or dietician. However, they can be involved with planning suitable meals, preparing shopping lists, cooking and coming up with new ideas to vary the healthy diet. Encourage structured meal times and make eating an occasion for talking and relaxing, rather than grabbing food on the move.

maintaining a diet plan

IT IS EASY to start a diet with good intentions, but difficult in practice to maintain it. Eating out and grabbing snacks on the run are real problems for many dieters, so it is important to understand exactly what you can eat. Keeping a diet interesting can also be difficult, so always look out for new suggestions.

It is not just the reasoning and theory behind a diet that is important but the practical issues that make it work. Planning meals in advance gives a diet structure and definitely promotes sensible choices, but this may not always be possible. Keeping carbohydrate intake under control may be a new and different way of eating, but it is not unusual and should not be too difficult. Starchy sources of carbohydrate, such as rice, potatoes, pasta and bread, should be avoided completely, and there are lots of alternatives for a filling and healthy diet. A meal consisting of protein, such as lean meat, poultry or fish, with two or three different vegetables or salad, is always an excellent and nutritious choice.

Below: *Large flat mushrooms baked with crushed garlic and olive oil are a simple yet delicious vegetable accompaniment.*

IDEAS FOR VEGETABLES

Vegetables can be shredded and stir-fried or cooked by many other methods instead of being boiled. Steaming vegetables or lightly stir-frying vegetable strips retains the goodness and fresh flavour. For a different texture, try coarsely grating vegetables such as carrots and cucumber.

- Large mushrooms can be baked with a spot of olive oil or pesto and used as a base for serving grilled meats, or served as an accompaniment.
- Courgettes (zucchini), (bell) peppers, aubergines (eggplant), carrots and tomatoes are delicious roasted – cooking this way intensifies their flavours.
- Beetroot (beet) and tomatoes can be dressed in balsamic vinegar.
- Bake courgettes, onions and aubergines in a rich garlic and tomato sauce.

Above: *Add interest to a simple bowl of mixed salad with extras such as chopped fruit, cold meat, grated cheese or nuts.*

- Bake leeks in a low-fat cheese sauce seasoned with mustard.
- Beans and lentils make a delicious base for meat or fish, or they can be cooked with spices and served as the main dish with vegetables or salad.
- Different types of salad leaves can be mixed to vary flavours and colours. For interest, introduce stronger flavours with watercress or rocket (arugula).
- A large bowl of mixed salad is an ideal dish. Nuts, peas, beans and lentils, such as chickpeas or kidney beans, grated or chopped vegetables, chopped apples, grated cheese, lean meat or fish can be added in whatever combinations you like. Toss with a small amount of dressing based on olive oil or low-fat yogurt to keep the calories down but avoid overwhelming the fresh ingredients by drenching them with dressing.

ALTERNATIVES TO SANDWICHES

Hot or cold soups can be carried in a flask to make a filling and nutritious meal. A large mixed salad can be carried to work in a sealed container, especially if there is a refrigerator to store food.

Instead of using bread, wrap low-fat cheeses or pates in cold ham or smoked salmon and cut into bitesize pieces. These are excellent with salad.

If there is no alternative, open sandwiches can be prepared on wholemeal bread sliced very thinly – try lean meat, fish or vegetables as a topping. Wraps using soft tortillas can hold lots of filling, while a taco shell is useful for scooping up dips, such as hummus or tzatsiki. Taco shells can be filled with salad for a crunchy snack, and sticks of carrot, cucumber and other vegetables are also good with dips.

SNACK IDEAS

If you need a snack between meals, this is not a bad thing, but remember to differentiate between boredom and hunger. Traditional snacks can be high in energy and low in nutrients so choose from these alternatives:

- Fresh fruit, such as melon wedges or chopped pineapple.
- Unsalted nuts in small amounts.
- Seeds, such as sunflower or pumpkin.
- Vegetable sticks on their own or to use with dips.

- Olives with cucumber sticks.
- Cheese fingers in small quantities.
- Yogurt – use natural as a base for mixing in prepared fruit to avoid the refined carbohydrates in flavoured yogurts.
- Fruit smoothies – whizz them up in a blender in seconds.

EATING OUT

From breakfast on the way to work, a snack at lunchtime or a main meal in the evening, eating out is no longer reserved for special occasions and treats.

American studies have shown that portion sizes have grown, with a cheeseburger increasing in weight from 162g in 1977 to 198g in 1996. The body quickly adjusts to these larger portion sizes, so the danger is that bigger meals may then be served at home.

Drinks are also getting larger. Red wine glasses are now usually 175ml rather than the traditional 125ml, and a shot of spirits has increased from 25ml to 35ml. Not only does this mean more calories but also more alcohol, which makes calculations of units consumed very confusing.

Sensible selections and an awareness of portions and quantities are important when eating out. Sharing dishes is a good way of distributing larger portions, and this is quite acceptable in most restaurants. In Chinese and Japanese restaurants, eating with chopsticks slows down eating and tends to limit the quantity consumed.

Indian food This can be very oily and high in energy. Choose tikka or tandoori meats or fish baked with spices and served with salad. Raita, a yogurt and cucumber dish, or a spicy dish of chopped onions with chilli are good accompaniments. Lassi, a flavoured buttermilk drink, is suitable but choose those flavoured with herbs or spices. Pulses can be a good choice and are delicious served with onions, tomato and yogurt. Indian sweets are high in refined sugars so avoid them.

Left: *Serve vegetable sticks with fresh dips based on cottage cheese or yogurt, for example with garlic and herbs.*

Above: *The average glass of wine served in restaurants today is larger than in the past, which means more calories.*

Italian food For an appetizer, choose Parma ham with melon, tricolore salad, stuffed mushrooms, tuna with beans, hearty bean and vegetable soups or traditional antipasto misto. Grilled meat or fish and salad or vegetables are good choices for the main course. Avoid pasta, risotto or pizza.

Chinese and East-Asian food Traditional soups with shredded meats, seafood and vegetables are a meal in one bowl, but soups thickened with starch or containing noodles should be avoided. Lettuce leaves are used as wraps for shredded meats and vegetables. Crispy Beijing duck is suitable as the pancakes contain as little as 4.5g carbohydrate each. Spare ribs or satay prawns, beef or chicken are good choices. Stir-fried vegetables are used as a base for many dishes, but some come in thickened sauces. Steamed fish is popular and tofu is an excellent alternative to meat or fish.

Turkish and Greek food This is mainly based on grilled meat or fish, served with salad, which is ideal. Be careful with dips, such as hummus, as these may be generously dressed with oil.

Mexican food Guacamole with grilled meat or fish is suitable. Choose salads and salsas, and mild jalapeno chillies or (bell) peppers. Fajitas and refried beans are fine but limit the number of taco shells or tortilla wraps. Avoid tortilla chips with sour cream and deep-fried tortillas.

breakfasts

FOR GOOD HEALTH, A SUSTAINING breakfast is an essential start to the day. Many classic breakfast foods, such as cereal or bagels, which can contain large amounts of carbohydrate, are simply not an option on a low-carbohydrate diet. However, there are lots of other quick, simple and nutritious choices that are just as tasty. Try combining one or two of the breakfast basics, or make the most of weekend mornings by enjoying a leisurely breakfast of poached eggs Florentine or herrings in oatmeal with bacon.

strawberry and honey smoothie

THIS ENERGIZING BLEND is simply bursting with goodness. Not only is tofu a good source of protein, it is also rich in minerals and contains nutrients that protect against diseases.

Makes 2 glasses

250g/9oz firm tofu
200g/7oz/1¾ cups strawberries
45ml/3 tbsp pumpkin or sunflower seeds, plus extra for sprinkling
30–45ml/2–3 tbsp clear honey
juice of 2 large oranges
juice of 1 lemon

NUTRITION NOTES

Per portion:	
Energy	325kcal/1368kJ
Protein	15.7g
Fat	13.7g
saturated fat	2.5g
Carbohydrate	38.8g
Fibre	3.2g
Calcium	90mg

1 Roughly chop the tofu, then hull the strawberries and chop them. Reserve a few strawberry chunks for garnish.

2 Put all of the ingredients into a blender or food processor and blend until completely smooth and creamy, scraping the mixture down from the side of the bowl, if necessary.

3 Pour into tumblers and sprinkle with extra seeds and strawberry chunks.

COOK'S TIP

Almost any other fruit can be used instead of the strawberries. Those that blend well, such as mangoes, bananas, peaches, plums and raspberries, are good substitutes.

egg-stuffed tomatoes

THIS SIMPLE DISH is just the kind of thing you might find in a charcuterie in France. It is easy to prepare at home and makes a light and nutritious breakfast or a simple lunch.

Serves 4

175ml/6fl oz/¾ cup low-fat crème fraiche
30ml/2 tbsp chopped fresh chives
30ml/2 tbsp chopped fresh basil
30ml/2 tbsp chopped fresh parsley
4 hard-boiled eggs
4 ripe tomatoes
salt and ground black pepper
salad leaves, to serve

1 In a small bowl, mix together the crème fraiche and herbs, and then set aside. Using an egg slicer or sharp knife, cut the eggs into thin slices, taking care to keep the slices intact.

2 Make deep cuts to within 1cm/½in of the base of each tomato. (There should be the same number of cuts in each tomato as there are slices of egg.)

NUTRITION NOTES

Per portion:	
Energy	99kcal/416kJ
Protein	9.8g
Fat	5.5g
saturated fat	1.8g
Carbohydrate	2.6g
Fibre	0.5g
Calcium	31mg

3 Fan open the tomatoes and sprinkle with salt, then insert an egg slice into each slit. Place each stuffed tomato on a plate with a few salad leaves, season and serve with the freshly prepared herb and crème fraiche mixture.

COOK'S TIP

For the best flavour, use the freshest, ripest tomatoes you can find.

savoury scrambled eggs

HIGH IN PROTEIN and low in carbohydrate, these tasty scrambled eggs make a nutritious breakfast that will keep you going throughout the morning.

Serves 2

2 slices wholegrain bread
25g/1oz/2 tbsp butter
2 eggs and 2 egg yolks, beaten
60–90ml/4–6 tbsp semi-skimmed (low-fat) milk
salt and ground black pepper
anchovy fillets, cut into strips, and paprika, to garnish
anchovy paste or Gentleman's Relish, for spreading

1 Toast the bread, then remove the crusts and cut the toast into triangles or squares, if you like. Keep warm.

2 Meanwhile, melt the butter in a pan over a very low heat.

3 Pour the eggs and milk into the butter and stir in a little salt and pepper. Heat very gently, stirring constantly, until the mixture begins to thicken. Remove the pan from the heat and continue to stir until the mixture becomes very creamy.

4 Place the toast on two plates and divide the eggs equally among them. Garnish each portion with strips of anchovy fillet and a generous sprinkling of paprika. Serve immediately, with anchovy paste to spread on the toast.

NUTRITION NOTES

Per portion:	
Energy	220kcal/919kJ
Protein	13.7g
Fat	13.3g
saturated fat	3.8g
Carbohydrate	13.0g
Fibre	1.1g
Calcium	112mg

soufflé omelette with mushrooms

A LIGHT, MOUTH-WATERING omelette makes a great morning meal. Mushrooms contain barely any carbohydrate, but are wonderfully satisfying and a source of B vitamins and minerals.

Serves 2
2 eggs, separated
15g/½oz/1 tbsp butter
flat leaf parsley or coriander (cilantro) leaves, to garnish

For the mushroom sauce
15g/½oz/1 tbsp butter
75g/3oz/generous 1 cup button (white) mushrooms, thinly sliced
15ml/1 tbsp plain (all-purpose) flour
75–120ml/2½–4fl oz/⅓–½ cup milk
5ml/1 tsp chopped fresh parsley (optional)
salt and ground black pepper

1 First, make the mushroom sauce. Melt the butter in a frying pan and add the sliced mushrooms. Cook gently over a low heat, stirring occasionally, for 4–5 minutes, until tender and juicy.

2 Stir the flour into the mushrooms, then slowly add the milk, stirring constantly. Bring to the boil and cook until thickened. Add the parsley, if using, and season with salt and pepper to taste. Keep warm.

3 Beat the egg yolks with 15ml/1 tbsp water and season with a little salt and pepper. Whisk the egg whites until stiff, then fold into the egg yolks using a metal spoon. Preheat the grill (broiler).

4 Melt the butter in a large frying pan and pour the egg mixture into the pan. Cook over a gentle heat for 2–3 minutes. Place the frying pan under the grill and cook for a further 2–3 minutes, until the top is golden brown.

5 Pour the mushroom sauce over the top of the omelette and fold it in half. Cut the omelette in half, and slide each portion on to a warmed plate. Serve immediately, garnished with parsley or coriander leaves.

NUTRITION NOTES

Per portion:	
Energy	244kcal/1020kJ
Protein	10.6g
Fat	17.5g
saturated fat	10.4g
Carbohydrate	8.5g
Fibre	0.7g
Calcium	106mg

poached eggs florentine

THE CLASSIC COMBINATION of eggs and spinach is high in protein and packed with vitamins and minerals. It is tasty and sustaining and makes an ideal weekend brunch if you have an active day ahead of you.

Serves 4
675g/1½lb spinach, washed and drained
pinch of freshly grated nutmeg
4 eggs
15ml/1 tbsp freshly grated Parmesan cheese, plus shavings to garnish
salt and ground black pepper

For the sauce
25g/1oz/2 tbsp butter
25g/1oz/¼ cup plain (all-purpose) flour
300ml/½ pint/1¼ cups hot milk
pinch of ground mace
115g/4oz/1 cup grated Gruyère cheese

VARIATION

To make a low-fat version of this dish, omit the Gruyère cheese from the recipe. It will work just as well.

1 Preheat the oven to 200°C/400°F/Gas 6. Place the spinach in a large pan with a little water. Cook for 3–4 minutes, then drain well and chop finely.

2 Return the spinach to the pan, add the nutmeg and seasoning and heat through. Spoon into four small gratin dishes, making a well in the middle of each.

3 To make the sauce, melt the butter in a small pan, add the flour and cook for 1 minute, stirring constantly. Gradually blend in the hot milk, beating well. Cook for 2 minutes, stirring constantly. Remove from the heat and stir in the mace and 75g/3oz/¾ cup of the Gruyère cheese.

4 Break each egg into a cup and slide into a pan of lightly salted simmering water. Poach for 3–4 minutes. Lift the eggs out using a slotted spoon and drain on kitchen paper.

5 Place a poached egg in the middle of each dish and cover with the sauce. Sprinkle with the remaining cheeses and bake for 10 minutes, or until just golden. Garnish with shavings of Parmesan cheese and serve immediately.

NUTRITION NOTES

Per portion:	
Energy	366kcal/1404kJ
Protein	25.9g
Fat	24.8g
saturated fat	12.4g
Carbohydrate	11.3g
Fibre	3.7g
Calcium	747mg

herrings in oatmeal with bacon

OILY FISH ARE AN EXCELLENT SOURCE of omega-3 fatty acids, which are essential for good health. They make a delicious, sustaining breakfast to take you through the day. For extra colour and flavour, serve with grilled tomatoes.

Serves 4

50g/2oz/½ cup medium oatmeal
10ml/2 tsp mustard powder
4 herrings, about 225g/8oz each, cleaned, boned, heads and tails removed
30ml/2 tbsp sunflower oil
8 rindless bacon rashers (strips)
salt and ground black pepper
lemon wedges, to serve

1 In a shallow dish, combine the oatmeal and mustard powder and season. Press the herrings in the mixture to coat.

2 Heat the oil in a large frying pan and fry the bacon until crisp. Drain on kitchen paper and keep hot.

3 Gently lay the herrings in the pan. You may need to cook them in two batches to avoid overcrowding the pan. Cook the fish for about 3–4 minutes on each side, until crisp and golden.

4 Using a fish slice (metal spatula), lift the herrings from the pan and place on warmed serving plates with the bacon rashers. Serve immediately with lemon wedges for squeezing over.

NUTRITION NOTES

Per portion:	
Energy	675kcal/2821kJ
Protein	48.7g
Fat	46.9g
saturated fat	11.4g
Carbohydrate	10.5g
Fibre	1.9g
Calcium	146mg

soups

LIGHT AND NUTRITIOUS SOUPS, whether served as a first course or as a simple lunch, can work perfectly as part of a low-carbohydrate diet. They are quick and simple to prepare, making it easy to include them as an essential part of your eating plan. Try making a large batch of your favourite soup and freezing individual portions, which can then be defrosted as you need them. Choose from traditional soups, such as creamy stilton and watercress soup or hearty chicken and avocado, or try something more exotic, such as miso broth with tofu.

lime and avocado soup

THIS DELICIOUS AND VERY PRETTY SOUP is perfect for dinner parties and has a fresh, delicate flavour. You might want to add a dash more lime juice just before serving for added zest.

Serves 4

2 large ripe avocados
300ml/½ pint/1 ¼ cups crème fraîche
1 litre/1 ¾ pints/4 cups well-flavoured chicken stock
5ml/1 tsp salt
juice of ½ lime
small bunch of coriander (cilantro)
ground black pepper

1 Halve the avocados, remove the stones (pits) and peel. Chop the flesh coarsely and process in a food processor with 3–4 tbsp of the crème fraîche until smooth.

2 Heat the chicken stock in a pan. When it is hot, but below simmering point, add the remaining crème fraîche and the salt.

3 Add the lime juice to the avocado mixture and process briefly to mix, then gradually stir the mixture into the hot chicken stock, ensuring it is thoroughly combined. Heat gently but do not let the mixture approach boiling point.

4 Roughly chop the coriander. Pour the soup into individual heated bowls and sprinkle each portion with chopped coriander and freshly ground black pepper. Serve immediately.

NUTRITION NOTES

Per portion:	
Energy	524kcal/2165kJ
Protein	6.8g
Fat	52.3g
saturated fat	22.3g
Carbohydrate	6.8g
Fibre	2.0g
Calcium	15mg

stilton and watercress soup

A GOOD CREAMY STILTON and plenty of fresh peppery watercress bring maximum flavour to this smooth soup. It is very rich so should be served in small portions.

Serves 6
600ml/1 pint/2½ cups vegetable stock
225g/8oz watercress
150g/5oz stilton or other blue cheese
150ml/¼ pint/⅔ cup plain yogurt

NUTRITION NOTES

Per portion:	
Energy	212kcal/884kJ
Protein	13.7g
Fat	15.5g
saturated fat	9.2g
Carbohydrate	4.9g
Fibre	1.9g
Calcium	326mg

1 Pour the vegetable stock into a pan and bring almost to the boil. Remove and discard any large stalks from the watercress. Add the watercress to the pan and simmer gently for about 2–3 minutes, until tender, being careful not to let it boil.

2 Crumble the cheese into the pan and simmer for 1 minute more, until the cheese has started to melt. Process the soup in a blender or food processor, in batches if necessary, until very smooth. Return the soup to the pan.

3 Stir in the yogurt and check the seasoning. The soup will probably not need any extra salt as the blue cheese is already quite salty. Heat the soup gently, without boiling, then ladle into warm bowls.

COOK'S TIP

Vegetarian varieties of some cheeses are available in large supermarkets and health food shops.

chicken and avocado soup

ORGANIC AVOCADOS RIPEN NATURALLY over a longer period of time, producing really rich-flavoured fruit. Here they add a creaminess to this delicious soup.

Serves 6

1.5 litres/2½ pints/6¼ cups chicken stock
½ fresh chilli, seeded
2 skinless, boneless chicken breast fillets
1 avocado
4 spring onions (scallions), finely sliced
400g/14oz can chickpeas, drained
sea salt and ground black pepper

1 Pour the chicken stock into a large pan and add the chilli. Bring to the boil, add the whole chicken breast fillets, then lower the heat and simmer for about 10 minutes, or until the chicken is cooked.

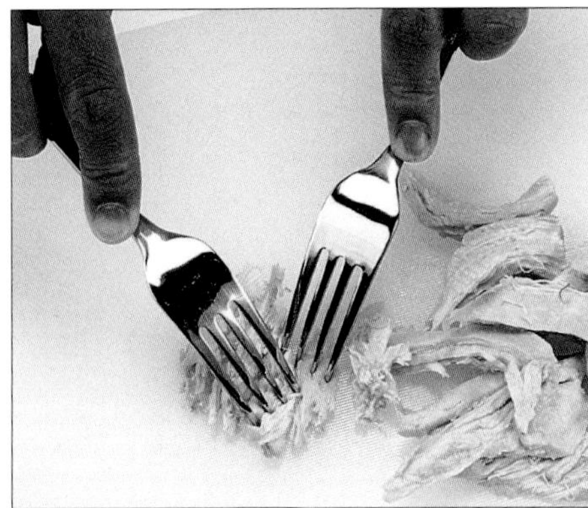

2 Remove the pan from the heat and lift out the chicken breasts with a slotted spoon. Leave to cool a little, then, using two forks, shred the chicken into small pieces. Set the shredded chicken aside.

3 Pour the chicken stock into a food processor or blender and add the chilli. Process the mixture until smooth, then return to the pan.

4 Cut the avocado in half, remove the skin and stone (pit) with a sharp knife, then slice the flesh into 2cm/¾in pieces. Add it to the stock, with the sliced spring onions and chickpeas.

5 Return the shredded chicken to the pan, add salt and freshly ground black pepper to taste, then heat gently. When the soup is heated through, spoon into warmed bowls and serve immediately.

NUTRITION NOTES

Per portion:	
Energy	146kcal/613kJ
Protein	12.3g
Fat	6.6g
saturated fat	1.1g
Carbohydrate	9.2g
Fibre	2.0g
Calcium	26mg

COOK'S TIP

Handle chillies with care as they can irritate the skin and eyes.

fragrant thai fish soup

LIGHT AND AROMATIC – and with virtually no carbohydrate – this is a perfect lunch or dinner dish. It is an excellent source of low-fat protein and contains essential nutrients for good health.

Serves 3
1 litre/1¾ pints/4 cups fish stock
4 lemon grass stalks
3 limes
2 small fresh hot red chillies, seeded and thinly sliced
2cm/¾in piece fresh galangal, peeled and thinly sliced
6 coriander (cilantro) stalks, with leaves
2 kaffir lime leaves, coarsely chopped (optional)
350g/12oz monkfish fillet, skinned and cut into 2.5cm/1in pieces
15ml/1 tbsp rice vinegar
45ml/3 tbsp Thai fish sauce
30ml/2 tbsp chopped fresh coriander (cilantro) leaves, to garnish

1 Pour the stock into a large pan and bring to the boil. Slice the bulb ends of the lemon grass diagonally into 3mm/⅛in thick pieces. Peel off four wide strips of lime rind with a vegetable peeler, avoiding the white pith. Squeeze the limes and reserve the juice.

2 Add the lemon grass, lime rind, chillies, galangal and coriander stalks to the stock, with the kaffir lime leaves, if using. Simmer for 1–2 minutes.

3 Add the monkfish, vinegar, fish sauce and half the reserved lime juice. Simmer for 3 minutes, until the fish is just cooked.

4 Remove the coriander stalks from the pan and discard. Taste the broth and add more lime juice if necessary. Serve the soup very hot, sprinkled with the chopped coriander leaves.

VARIATION

Other fish or shellfish such as sole, prawns (shrimp), scallops or squid can be substituted for the monkfish.

NUTRITION NOTES

Per portion:	
Energy	116Kcal/484kJ
Protein	25.8g
Fat	0.7g
saturated fat	0.2g
Carbohydrate	0.1g
Fibre	0g
Calcium	17.4mg

miso broth with tofu

THIS FLAVOURSOME BROTH is simple and highly nutritious. In Japan, it is traditionally eaten for breakfast, but it also makes a good appetizer, light lunch or supper.

Serves 4

- 1 bunch of spring onions (scallions) or 5 baby leeks
- 15g/½oz fresh coriander (cilantro)
- 3 thin slices fresh root ginger
- 2 star anise
- 1 small dried red chilli
- 1.2 litres/2 pints/5 cups dashi or vegetable stock
- 225g/8oz pak choi (bok choy) or other Asian greens, thickly sliced
- 200g/7oz firm tofu, cut into 2.5cm/1in cubes
- 60ml/4 tbsp red miso
- 30–45ml/2–3 tbsp Japanese soy sauce
- 1 fresh red chilli, seeded and shredded (optional)

1 Cut the coarse green tops off the spring onions or baby leeks and slice the rest of the spring onions or leeks finely on the diagonal. Place the coarse green tops in a large pan with the stalks from the coriander, the fresh root ginger, star anise, dried chilli and dashi or vegetable stock.

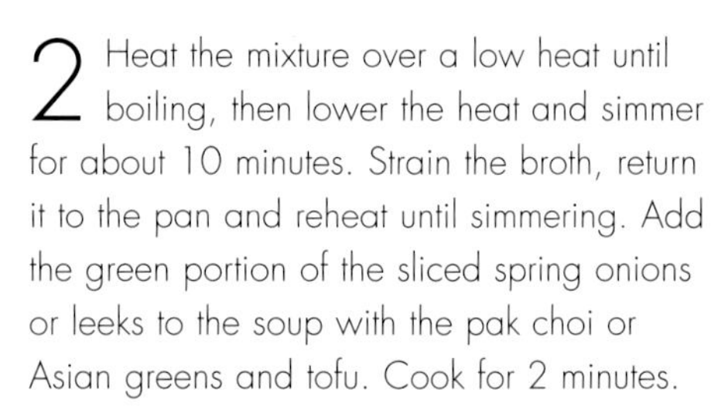

2 Heat the mixture over a low heat until boiling, then lower the heat and simmer for about 10 minutes. Strain the broth, return it to the pan and reheat until simmering. Add the green portion of the sliced spring onions or leeks to the soup with the pak choi or Asian greens and tofu. Cook for 2 minutes.

3 In a small bowl, combine the miso with a little soup, then stir the mixture into the pan. Add soy sauce to taste.

4 Coarsely chop the coriander leaves and stir most of them into the soup with the white part of the spring onions or leeks.

5 Cook for 1 minute, then ladle the soup into warmed bowls. Sprinkle with the remaining chopped coriander and the shredded fresh red chilli, if using, and serve immediately.

NUTRITION NOTES

Per portion:	
Energy	72Kcal/300kJ
Protein	7.2g
Fat	3.1g
saturated fat	0.4g
Carbohydrate	4.2g
Fibre	3.4g
Calcium	374mg

fish and egg-knot soup

TWISTS OF OMELETTE and steamed prawn balls add protein and substance to this light Asian soup. It is the perfect appetizer before a low-carbohydrate main course.

Serves 4
1 spring onion (scallion), finely shredded
800ml/1⅓ pints/3½ cups well-flavoured stock or dashi
5ml/1 tsp soy sauce
dash of sake or dry white wine
pinch of salt

For the prawn balls
200g/7oz/generous 1 cup large raw prawns (shrimp), peeled, thawed if frozen
65g/2½oz cod fillet, skinned
5ml/1 tsp egg white
5ml/1 tsp sake or dry white wine, plus a dash extra
25ml/1½ tbsp cornflour (cornstarch) or potato flour
2–3 drops soy sauce
pinch of salt

For the omelette
1 egg, beaten
dash of mirin
pinch of salt
oil, for cooking

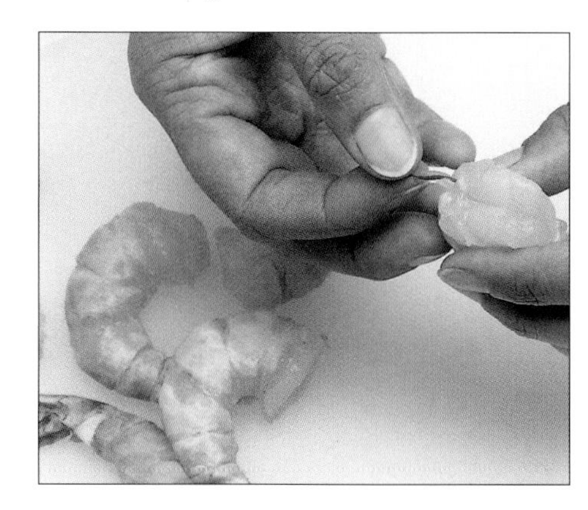

1 To make the prawn balls, use a pin to remove the black vein running down the back of each prawn. Place the prawns, cod, egg white, sake or dry white wine, cornflour or potato flour, soy sauce and a pinch of salt in a food processor or blender and process to a thick, sticky paste.

2 Shape the fish mixture into four balls, place in a steaming basket and steam over a pan of vigorously boiling water for about 10 minutes.

3 Soak the shredded spring onion in iced water for about 5 minutes, until the shreds curl. Drain and set aside.

4 To make the omelette, combine the egg, mirin and salt. Heat a little oil in a frying pan and pour in the egg and mirin mixture, coating the pan evenly. When the omelette has set, turn it over and cook for 30 seconds. Slide out and leave to cool, then cut the omelette into strips and tie each in a knot.

5 Heat the stock or dashi, then add the soy sauce, wine and salt. Divide the prawn balls and egg-knots among four bowls and add the soup. Serve with the onion curls.

NUTRITION NOTES

Per portion:	
Energy	94kcal/392kJ
Protein	13.8g
Fat	2.3g
saturated fat	0.6g
Carbohydrate	5.3g
Fibre	0g
Calcium	54mg

appetizers

GET ANY MEAL OFF TO A GOOD start with these delicious, low-carbohydrate appetizers. However, try to avoid heavy, three-course meals in the evening – unless, of course, you are entertaining, in which case you should spoil yourself. There is no need to compromise on flavour with dishes such as pink grapefruit and avocado salad or carpaccio with rocket, which could also be enjoyed as a light lunch. Other recipes in this chapter, including garlic prawns, and bacon-rolled enokitake mushrooms, make irresistible finger food at parties.

cheese and tomato soufflés

GUESTS ARE ALWAYS IMPRESSED by a home-made soufflé and this recipe for little individual ones is the ultimate in effortless entertaining. Just don't tell them you used a ready-made sauce.

Serves 6

350g/12oz tub fresh cheese sauce
50g/2oz sun-dried tomatoes in olive oil, drained, plus 10ml/2 tsp of the oil
130g/4½oz/1½ cups grated Parmesan cheese
4 large (US extra large) eggs, separated
salt and ground black pepper

NUTRITION NOTES

Per portion:	
Energy	270kcal/1125kJ
Protein	16.7g
Fat	20.3g
saturated fat	9.6g
Carbohydrate	5.7g
Fibre	0.4g
Calcium	435mg

1 Preheat the oven to 200°C/400°F/Gas 6. Tip the cheese sauce into a bowl. Thinly slice the sun-dried tomatoes and add them to the sauce with 90g/3½oz/generous 1 cup of the Parmesan cheese and the egg yolks. Season well with salt and black pepper and stir until thoroughly combined.

2 Brush the base and sides of six 200ml/7fl oz/scant 1 cup ramekins or individual soufflé dishes with the oil, then divide about half of the remaining Parmesan cheese among the dishes. Coat the insides of the dishes with the cheese, tilting them until evenly covered. Tip out any excess cheese and set aside with the reserved cheese.

3 Whisk the egg whites in a clean, grease-free bowl until stiff. Use a large metal spoon to stir one-quarter of the egg whites into the sauce, stirring gently until evenly blended, then fold in the remaining egg whites.

4 Spoon the mixture into the prepared ramekins or soufflé dishes and sprinkle with the reserved cheese. Place the ramekins on a baking sheet and bake for about 15–18 minutes, or until the soufflé is well risen and golden. Serve immediately with a mixed green salad.

chilli egg rolls

THE TITLE OF THIS RECIPE could lead to some confusion. However, these are not Chinese egg rolls; they are wedges of a rolled Thai-flavoured omelette, perfect as finger food.

Serves 2
3 eggs, beaten
15ml/1 tbsp soy sauce
1 bunch garlic chives, thinly sliced
1–2 small fresh red or green chillies, seeded and finely chopped
small bunch fresh coriander (cilantro), chopped
pinch of granulated sugar
salt and ground black pepper
15ml/1 tbsp groundnut (peanut) oil

For the dipping sauce
60ml/4 tbsp light soy sauce
fresh lime juice, to taste

1 Make the dipping sauce. Pour the soy sauce into a bowl. Add a generous squeeze of lime juice. Taste and add more lime juice if needed.

2 Mix the eggs, soy sauce, chives, chillies and coriander. Add the sugar and season to taste. Heat the oil in a large frying pan, pour in the egg mixture and swirl the pan to make an omelette.

COOK'S TIP
After preparing chillies, wash your hands thoroughly in warm, soapy water.

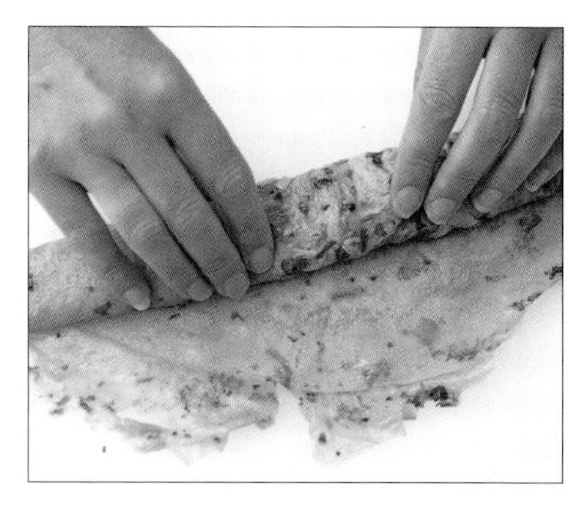

3 Cook for 1–2 minutes, until the omelette is just firm and the underside is turning golden. Slide it out on to a plate and roll up as though it were a pancake. Leave to cool completely.

4 When the omelette is cool, slice it diagonally in 1cm/½in pieces. Arrange the slices on a serving platter and serve with the bowl of dipping sauce.

NUTRITION NOTES

Per portion:	
Energy	218kcal/907kJ
Protein	11.4g
Fat	16.0g
saturated fat	4.0g
Carbohydrate	6.1g
Fibre	0
Calcium	67mg

baked eggs with creamy leeks

THIS SIMPLE BUT ELEGANT APPETIZER is perfect for last-minute entertaining or quick dining. Garnish the baked eggs with crisp, freshly fried sage leaves and serve for a special meal.

Serves 4

15g/½oz/1 tbsp butter, plus extra for greasing
225g/8oz small leeks, thinly sliced
75–90ml/5–6 tbsp whipping cream
4 small-medium (US medium-large) eggs

1 Preheat the oven to 190°C/375°F/Gas 5. Generously butter the base and sides of four small ramekins or individual soufflé dishes.

NUTRITION NOTES

Per portion:	
Energy	193kcal/800kJ
Protein	7.7g
Fat	16.4g
saturated fat	8.3g
Carbohydrate	4.0g
Fibre	1.7g
Calcium	76mg

2 Melt the butter in a frying pan and cook the leeks over a medium heat, stirring frequently, for 3–5 minutes, until softened and translucent, but not browned.

3 Add 45ml/3 tbsp of the cream and cook over a low heat for 5 minutes, until the leeks are very soft and the cream has thickened a little. Season to taste.

4 Place the ramekins in a small roasting pan and divide the cooked leeks among them. Break an egg into each, spoon over the remaining cream and season with salt and pepper.

5 Pour boiling water into the roasting pan to come about halfway up the sides of the ramekins. Transfer the pan to the preheated oven and bake for about 10 minutes, until just set. Serve piping hot.

pink grapefruit and avocado salad

CREAMY AVOCADO AND ZESTY CITRUS FRUITS combine in this refreshing salad. Avocados turn brown quickly when exposed to the air, but the grapefruit juice will prevent this from occurring.

Serves 4
2 pink grapefruits
2 ripe avocados
30ml/2 tbsp chilli oil
90g/3½oz rocket (arugula)

1 Slice the top and bottom off one of the grapefruits, then cut off all of the peel and pith from around the side – the best way to do this is to cut down in wide strips. Working over a small bowl to catch the juices, carefully cut out the segments from between the membranes and place them in a separate bowl. Squeeze any juices remaining in the membranes into the bowl, then discard them. Repeat with the remaining grapefruit.

2 Halve, stone (pit) and peel both of the avocados. Slice the flesh and add it to the grapefruit segments. Whisk a pinch of salt into the grapefruit juice, followed by the chilli oil.

3 Pile the rocket leaves on to four plates and top with the grapefruit segments and avocado slices. Pour over the dressing and toss slightly with your hands, then serve immediately.

NUTRITION NOTES

Per portion:	
Energy	252kcal/1050kJ
Protein	4.1g
Fat	23.7g
saturated fat	3.0g
Carbohydrate	6.4g
Fibre	1.9g
Calcium	61mg

bacon-rolled enokitake mushrooms

THE JAPANESE NAME FOR THIS DISH is *obimaki enoki*. The strong, smoky flavour of the bacon complements the subtle flavour of the mushrooms. Small heaps of ground white pepper can be offered with these savouries, if you like.

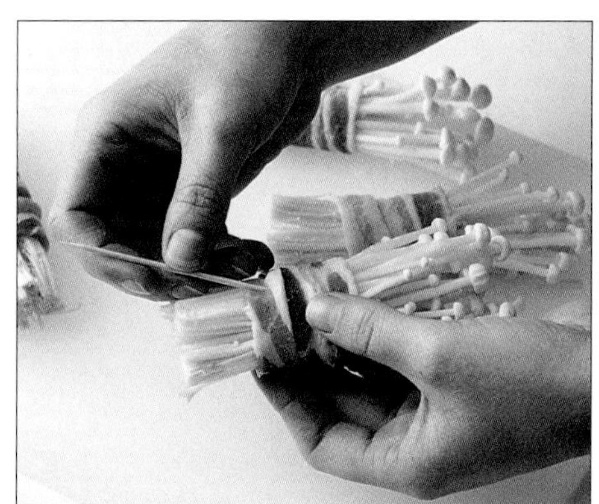

Serves 4

- 450g/1lb fresh enokitake mushrooms
- 6 rindless smoked streaky (fatty) bacon rashers (strips)
- 4 lemon wedges

1 Cut off the root part of each enokitake cluster 2cm/¾in from the end. Do not separate the stems. Cut the bacon rashers in half lengthways.

2 Divide the enokitake into 12 equal bunches. Take one bunch, then place the middle of the enokitake mushroom near the edge of one bacon rasher, with approximately 2.5–4cm/1–1½in of enokitake protruding at each end.

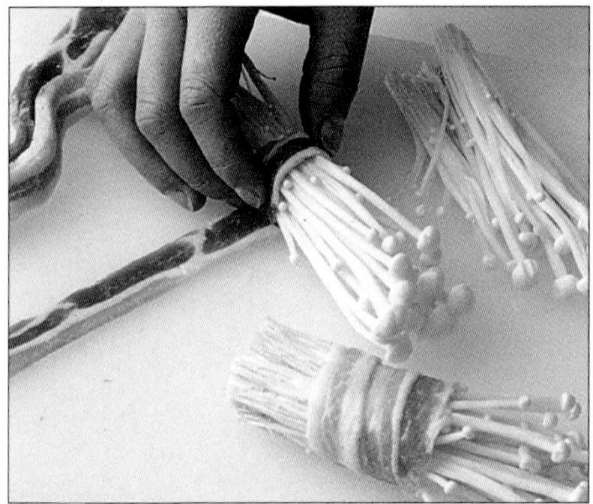

3 Carefully roll up the bunch of enokitake in the bacon. Tuck any straying short stems into the bacon and slide the bacon slightly upwards to cover about 4cm/1½in of the enokitake.

4 Secure the end of the bacon roll by skewering it with a cocktail stick (toothpick). Repeat using the remaining enokitake and bacon to make 11 more rolls. Preheat the grill (broiler) to high, and place the enokitake rolls on an oiled wire rack. Grill (broil) both sides until the bacon is crisp and golden and the enokitake mushrooms start to char. This should take about 10–13 minutes.

5 Remove the enokitake rolls and place on a chopping board. Using a knife and fork, chop each roll in half through the middle of the bacon belt. Arrange the top part of the enokitake roll standing upright, with the bottom part lying down next to it. Add a thin wedge of lemon to each portion and serve.

NUTRITION NOTES

Per portion:	
Energy	221kcal/916kJ
Protein	9.3g
Fat	20.5g
saturated fat	8.1g
Carbohydrate	0g
Fibre	3.6g
Calcium	8mg

grilled spring greens with prosciutto

THIS IS A GOOD CHOICE OF FIRST COURSE at the beginning of summer, when both spring onions and asparagus are at their best. The slight smokiness of the grilled vegetables goes very well with the sweetness of the air-dried ham.

Serves 4
about 24 plump spring onions (scallions)
500g/1¼lb asparagus
45–60ml/3–4 tbsp olive oil
20ml/4 tsp balsamic vinegar
8–12 slices prosciutto
50g/2oz Pecorino cheese
sea salt and ground black pepper
extra virgin olive oil, to serve

1 Trim the root, outer papery skin and the top off the spring onions.

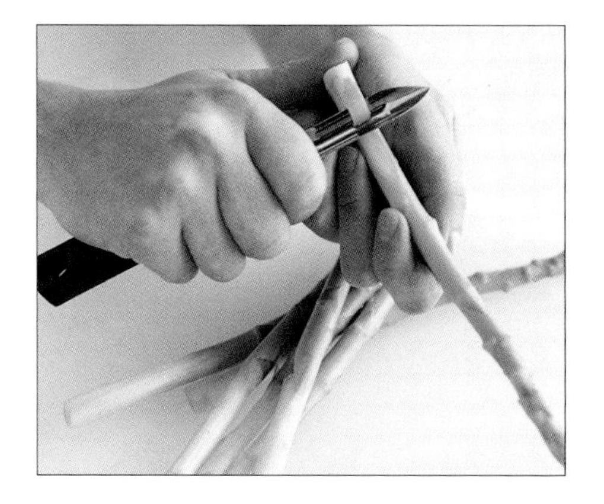

2 Cut off and discard the woody ends of the asparagus and peel the bottom 7.5cm/3in of the spears.

3 Heat the grill (broiler). Toss the spring onions and asparagus in 30ml/2 tbsp olive oil. Place on two baking sheets and season well with sea salt and freshly ground black pepper.

4 Grill (broil) the asparagus for 5 minutes on each side, until just tender when tested with the tip of a sharp knife. Protect the tips with foil if they begin to char too much. Grill the spring onions for about 3–4 minutes on each side, until tinged a slightly golden colour. Brush both vegetables with a little more oil when you turn them.

5 Distribute the vegetables among four to six plates. Season with black pepper and drizzle over the vinegar. Lay two to three slices of ham on each plate and shave the Pecorino over the top. Provide extra olive oil for drizzling at the table.

COOK'S TIP

The spring onions could be cooked on a cast-iron ridged griddle pan. If it is more convenient, the asparagus can be roasted at 200°C/400°F/Gas 6 for 15 minutes instead of grilled.

NUTRITION NOTES

Per portion:	
Energy	236kcal/983kJ
Protein	3.8g
Fat	15.8g
saturated fat	1.4g
Carbohydrate	5.0g
Fibre	2.9g
Calcium	90mg

carpaccio with rocket

A VENETIAN DISH, carpaccio is named in honour of the Renaissance painter. In this fine Italian dish raw beef is lightly dressed with lemon juice and olive oil and is traditionally served with flakes of Parmesan cheese.

Serves 4
1 garlic clove
1½ lemons
50ml/2fl oz/¼ cup extra virgin olive oil
2 bunches rocket (arugula)
4 very thin slices of beef fillet
115g/4oz Parmesan cheese, shaved
salt and ground black pepper

1 Cut the garlic clove in half with a small sharp knife, then rub the cut side over the inside of a large glass bowl. Squeeze the lemons into the bowl, then gradually whisk in the extra virgin olive oil. Season with plenty of salt and freshly ground black pepper, then leave to stand for at least 15 minutes.

2 Carefully wash the rocket and tear off any thick stalks. Pat dry with kitchen paper. Arrange the rocket around the edge of a large serving platter or divide among four individual plates.

3 Place the sliced beef in the centre of the platter, and pour the sauce over it, spreading it evenly over the meat. Arrange the shaved Parmesan on top of the meat slices and serve immediately.

NUTRITION NOTES

Per portion:	
Energy	281kcal/1174kJ
Protein	17.6g
Fat	22.7g
saturated fat	7.5g
Carbohydrate	2.3g
Fibre	0.2g
Calcium	427mg

garlic prawns

THIS WONDERFUL, BUT SIMPLE dish with its aroma of garlic and hint of chilli takes only minutes to cook, so it is perfect for entertaining. Serve it for a dinner party and your guests will never guess that you are following a diet.

Serves 4
350–450g/12oz–1lb raw prawns (shrimp)
2 fresh red chillies
45ml/3 tbsp olive oil
3 garlic cloves, crushed
salt and ground black pepper

1 Remove the heads and shells from the prawns, leaving the tails intact. Remove the dark vein along the back of the prawns with a sharp knife or a pin.

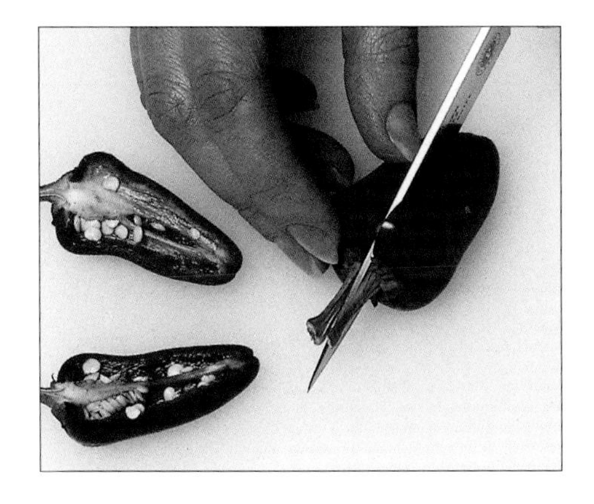

2 Halve each chilli lengthways and discard the seeds. Heat the oil in a flameproof pan, suitable for serving.

3 Add the prawns, chillies and garlic to the pan and cook over a high heat for 3 minutes, stirring constantly until the prawns turn pink. Season and serve immediately.

VARIATIONS

- To add extra spice, stir in 10ml/2 tsp finely chopped fresh root ginger with the chillies and garlic.
- To make a light lunch, serve the prawns on a bed of colourful mixed salad leaves and fresh herbs, such as coriander (cilantro) or mint.
- For a special occasion, use lobster tails or crawfish instead of prawns.

NUTRITION NOTES

Per portion:	
Energy	226kcal/944kJ
Protein	35g
Fat	9.4g
saturated fat	1.4g
Carbohydrate	0g
Fibre	0g
Calcium	44mg

main course salads

GENEROUS, LEAFY GREEN SALADS can easily be turned into a nutritious main meal with the addition of ingredients such as fish, tofu, nuts or meat. They are healthy and satisfying, offering essential fibre, nutrients and sustaining low-fat protein, which makes them perfect for a low-carbohydrate diet. All of the recipes in this chapter are simple to prepare, taste delicious and fit easily into your weekly menu and healthy eating plan. Try a simple salad with omelette strips and bacon or indulge in a delicious seafood or warm monkfish salad.

fried egg salad

CHILLIES AND EGGS MAY SEEM UNLIKELY PARTNERS, but they actually work well together. The peppery flavour of the watercress makes it the perfect foundation for this tasty salad.

Serves 2

15ml/1 tbsp groundnut (peanut) oil
1 garlic clove, thinly sliced
4 eggs
2 shallots, thinly sliced
2 small fresh red chillies, seeded and thinly sliced
½ small cucumber, finely diced
1cm/½in piece fresh root ginger, peeled and grated
juice of 2 limes
30ml/2 tbsp soy sauce
5ml/1 tsp caster (superfine) sugar
small bunch coriander (cilantro)
bunch watercress, coarsely chopped

1 Heat the oil in a frying pan. Add the garlic and cook over a low heat until it starts to turn golden. Crack in the eggs. Break the yolks with a wooden spatula, then fry until the eggs are almost firm. Remove from the pan and set aside.

2 Mix the shallots, chillies, cucumber and ginger in a bowl. In a separate bowl, whisk the lime juice with the soy sauce and caster sugar. Pour this dressing over the vegetables and toss lightly.

3 Set aside a few coriander sprigs for the garnish. Chop the rest and add to the salad. Toss it again.

4 Reserve a few watercress sprigs and arrange the remainder on two serving plates. Cut the fried eggs into slices and divide them between the watercress mounds. Spoon the shallot mixture over them and serve, garnished with the reserved coriander and watercress.

NUTRITION NOTES

Per portion:	
Energy	521kcal/2179kJ
Protein	36.2g
Fat	20.7g
saturated fat	4.9g
Carbohydrate	11.5g
Fibre	1.3g
Calcium	407mg

greek salad

THIS WONDERFULLY TANGY SALAD makes a perfect lunch or supper dish. The ingredients offer a range of nutrients, from vitamins C and E to monounsaturated fats and protein.

Serves 4

1 small cos or romaine lettuce, sliced
450g/1lb well-flavoured tomatoes, cut into eighths
1 cucumber, seeded and chopped
200g/7oz feta cheese, crumbled
4 spring onions (scallions), sliced
50g/2oz/½ cup black olives, pitted and halved

For the dressing

45ml/3 tbsp olive oil
25ml/1½ tbsp lemon juice
salt and ground black pepper

NUTRITION NOTES

Per portion:	
Energy	240kcal/1002kJ
Protein	9.5g
Fat	20.4g
saturated fat	8.4g
Carbohydrate	5.4g
Fibre	2.3g
Calcium	210mg

1 Put the lettuce, tomatoes, cucumber, crumbled feta cheese, spring onions and olives in a large salad bowl.

2 For the dressing, whisk together the olive oil and lemon juice, then season. Pour over the salad, toss well and serve.

salad with omelette strips and bacon

CRISP BACON AND HERBY OMELETTE STRIPS add substance and protein to this light and tasty salad.

Serves 4
- 6 streaky (fatty) bacon rashers (strips), rinds removed and chopped
- 400g/14oz mixed salad leaves, including some distinctively flavoured leaves such as rocket (arugula), watercress and fresh herbs
- 2 eggs
- 2 spring onions (scallions), chopped
- few sprigs of coriander (cilantro), chopped
- 25g/1oz/2 tbsp butter
- 60ml/4 tbsp olive oil
- 30ml/2 tbsp balsamic vinegar
- salt and ground black pepper

1 Warm an omelette pan over a low heat. Add the chopped bacon and cook gently until the fat runs. Increase the heat to crisp the bacon, stirring frequently. When the bacon pieces are brown and crispy, remove from the heat and transfer to a hot dish to keep warm.

2 Place the salad leaves in a large bowl. In another bowl, beat the eggs with the chopped spring onions and coriander and season well with salt and pepper.

3 Melt the butter in the omelette pan and pour in the eggs. Cook for about 3 minutes to make an unfolded omelette. Cut into long strips and keep warm.

4 Add the oil, vinegar and seasoning to the pan and heat briefly. Sprinkle the bacon and omelette strips over the salad leaves, then pour over the dressing. Toss.

NUTRITION NOTES

Per portion:	
Energy	321kcal/1341kJ
Protein	13.4g
Fat	28.9g
saturated fat	9.0g
Carbohydrate	2.2g
Fibre	0.9g
Calcium	49mg

chilli salad omelettes with hummus

THESE DELICATE OMELETTES filled with healthy and nutritious salad make a refreshing low-carbohydrate lunch.

Serves 4
- 4 eggs
- 15ml/1 tbsp cornflour (cornstarch)
- 115g/4oz/1 cup shredded salad vegetables
- 60ml/4 tbsp chilli salad dressing
- 60–75ml/4–5 tbsp hummus
- 4 cooked bacon rashers (strips), chopped
- salt and ground black pepper

NUTRITION NOTES

Per portion:	
Energy	358kcal/1498kJ
Protein	19.1g
Fat	29.1g
saturated fat	6.8g
Carbohydrate	6.2g
Fibre	0.8g
Calcium	54mg

1 Beat together the eggs, cornflour and 15ml/1 tbsp water. Heat a lightly oiled frying pan and pour a quarter of the mixture into the pan, tipping it to spread it out evenly. Cook the omelette gently. When cooked, remove from the pan, then make 3 more omelettes. Stack them between sheets of baking parchment, then chill.

2 When ready to serve, toss the shredded salad vegetables together with about 45ml/3 tbsp of the dressing.

3 Spread half of each omelette with hummus, top with the salad vegetables and chopped bacon and fold in half. Drizzle the rest of the dressing over the filled omelettes before serving.

warm monkfish salad

GRIDDLED MONKFISH tossed with nutritious pine nuts and vitamin-rich baby spinach is a delicious combination that will make you forget you are on a diet.

Serves 4
2 monkfish fillets, each weighing about 350g/12oz
25g/1oz/¼ cup pine nuts
15ml/1 tbsp olive oil
225g/8oz baby spinach leaves, washed and stalks removed
salt and ground black pepper

For the dressing
5ml/1 tsp Dijon mustard
5ml/1 tsp sherry vinegar
30ml/2 tbsp olive oil
1 garlic clove, crushed

VARIATION

Substitute salad leaves for the spinach if you like. Watercress and rocket (arugula) would be good alternatives.

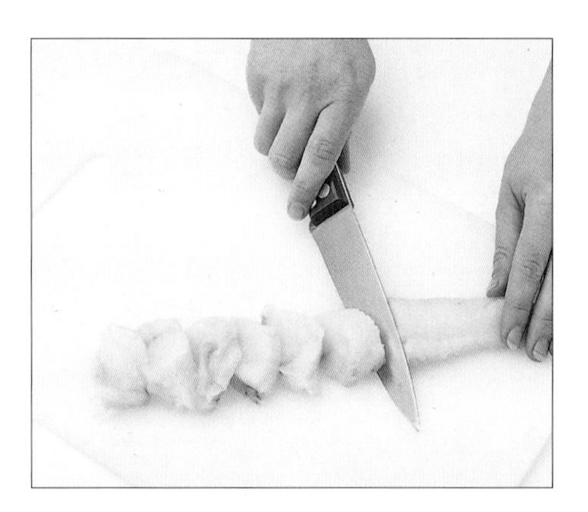

1 Holding the knife at a slight angle, cut each monkfish fillet into 12 diagonal slices. Season lightly and set aside.

2 Heat a dry frying pan, put in the pine nuts and shake them over a low heat, until golden brown but not burned. Transfer to a plate and set aside.

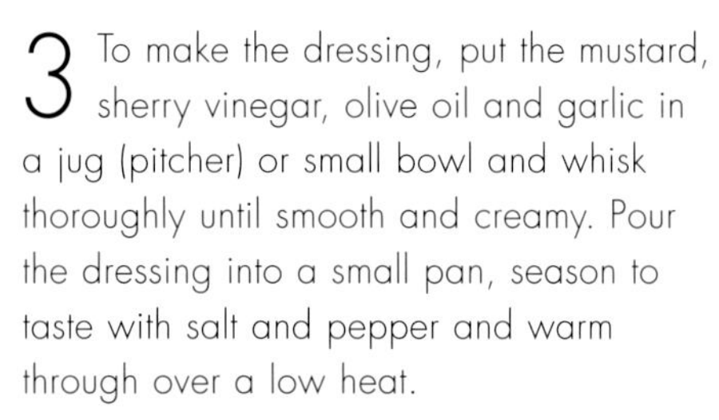

3 To make the dressing, put the mustard, sherry vinegar, olive oil and garlic in a jug (pitcher) or small bowl and whisk thoroughly until smooth and creamy. Pour the dressing into a small pan, season to taste with salt and pepper and warm through over a low heat.

4 Heat the oil in a ridged griddle pan or frying pan until sizzling. Add the fish slices and sauté for about 20–30 seconds on each side.

5 Put the spinach leaves into a large bowl and pour over the warm salad dressing. Sprinkle on the toasted pine nuts, reserving a few, and toss together well. Divide the dressed spinach leaves among four serving plates and arrange the fish slices on top. Sprinkle over the reserved pine nuts and serve immediately.

NUTRITION NOTES

Per portion:	
Energy	222kcal/927kJ
Protein	29.9g
Fat	10.9g
saturated fat	1.3g
Carbohydrate	1.1g
Fibre	1.3g
Calcium	110mg

seafood salad

CRISP SALAD LEAVES and fresh shellfish are a tasty combination that fit perfectly within a diet because both are naturally low in carbohydrate. Vary the seafood depending on what is available.

Serves 6
450g/1lb live mussels, scrubbed and bearded
450g/1lb small clams, scrubbed
105ml/7 tbsp dry white wine
225g/8oz squid, cleaned
4 large scallops, with their corals
30ml/2 tbsp olive oil
2 garlic cloves, finely chopped
1 small dried red chilli, crumbled
225g/8oz cooked unpeeled prawns (shrimp)
6–8 large chicory (Belgian endive) leaves
6–8 radicchio leaves
15ml/1 tbsp chopped flat leaf parsley, to garnish

For the dressing
5ml/1 tsp Dijon mustard
30ml/2 tbsp white wine or cider vinegar
5ml/1 tsp lemon juice
75ml/5 tbsp extra virgin olive oil
salt and ground black pepper

1 Put the mussels and clams in a large pan and pour in the dry white wine. Cover tightly and cook over a high heat, shaking the pan occasionally, for about 4 minutes, until the shells have opened. Discard any that remain closed. Use a slotted spoon to transfer the shellfish to a bowl, then strain thoroughly and reserve the cooking liquid.

2 Cut the squid bodies into thin rings and chop the tentacles into bite-size pieces. Leave any small squid whole. Halve the scallops horizontally.

3 Heat the olive oil in a large frying pan. Add the chopped garlic, chilli, squid, scallops and their corals, and sauté gently over a low heat for about 2 minutes, until just cooked and tender. Lift the squid, scallops and corals out of the pan, reserving any oil that remains.

4 When the mussels and clams are cool, shell them, keeping 12 of each in the shell. Peel all but six of the prawns.

5 Strain the shellfish cooking liquid into a small pan, set over a high heat, bring to the boil and reduce by half. In a large bowl, combine all the mussels and clams with the squid and scallops, then add the prawns.

6 To make the dressing, whisk the Dijon mustard with the white wine or cider vinegar and lemon juice and season with salt and ground black pepper. Add the olive oil, whisk, then whisk in the cooking liquid and oil from the frying pan. Pour the dressing over the seafood mixture and toss lightly.

7 Arrange the salad leaves around the edge of a large serving dish and pile the seafood mixture into the centre of the dish. Sprinkle with the chopped parsley and serve immediately.

NUTRITION NOTES

Per portion:	
Energy	252kcal/1053kJ
Protein	26.5g
Fat	13.5g
saturated fat	2.2g
Carbohydrate	3.9g
Fibre	0.1g
Calcium	106mg

warm chicken and tomato salad

THIS SIMPLE, WARM SALAD combines pan-fried chicken breasts, cherry tomatoes and fresh baby spinach with a light, nutty dressing. Serve it for lunch on a cool autumn day.

Serves 4

45ml/3 tbsp olive oil
30ml/2 tbsp hazelnut oil
15ml/1 tbsp white wine vinegar
1 garlic clove, crushed
15ml/1 tbsp chopped fresh mixed herbs
225g/8oz baby spinach leaves
250g/9oz cherry tomatoes, halved
1 bunch spring onions (scallions), chopped
2 skinless chicken breast portions, cut into thin strips
salt and ground black pepper

VARIATIONS

Instead of chicken, try using beef steak, pork fillet or even salmon fillet.

1 First make the dressing: place 30ml/2 tbsp of the olive oil, the hazelnut oil, vinegar, garlic and chopped herbs in a small bowl or jug (pitcher) and whisk together until thoroughly mixed. Set aside.

2 Trim any long stalks from the baby spinach leaves, then place in a large serving bowl with the halved cherry tomatoes and chopped spring onions, and gently toss together to mix.

3 Heat the remaining olive oil in a frying pan, and stir-fry the chicken strips over a high heat for about 7–10 minutes, until they are cooked through. The chicken should be tender and lightly browned.

4 Arrange the cooked chicken pieces over the mixed salad. Give the dressing a quick whisk to make sure the ingredients are well mixed, then drizzle it over the salad, to taste. Season with salt and ground black pepper, toss lightly with your hands and serve immediately.

NUTRITION NOTES

Per portion:	
Energy	265kcal/1111kJ
Protein	14.8g
Fat	20.9g
saturated fat	3.1g
Carbohydrate	5.3g
Fibre	2.6g
Calcium	85mg

warm chorizo and spinach salad

IN THIS HEARTY WARM SALAD, spinach has sufficient flavour to compete with the spiciness of the chorizo. Try using a flavoured olive oil as well – rosemary, garlic or chilli oil would be perfect.

Serves 4
225g/8oz baby spinach leaves
45ml/3 tbsp extra virgin olive oil
150g/5oz chorizo sausage, very thinly sliced
30ml/2 tbsp sherry vinegar

NUTRITION NOTES

Per portion:	
Energy	287kcal/1200kJ
Protein	11.0g
Fat	25.8g
saturated fat	7.0g
Carbohydrate	2.8g
Fibre	1.3g
Calcium	57mg

1 Discard any tough stalks from the baby spinach leaves. Pour the oil into a large frying pan and add the sliced chorizo sausage. Cook gently for 3 minutes, until the sausage slices start to shrivel slightly and turn a darker colour.

2 Add the spinach leaves and remove the pan from the heat. Toss the spinach in the warm oil until it just starts to wilt. Add the sherry vinegar and a little seasoning. Toss the ingredients briefly, then serve immediately, while still warm.

meat and poultry

Hot meals are an essential part of most people's weekly menu, but they don't have to enter the danger zone of high-carbohydrate comfort food. Eat meat and poultry regularly for essential and filling proteins and fats. Whatever your taste, from hot and spicy to subtle and delicate, there is a perfect dish here, from stir-fried pork with dried shrimp to steak with warm tomato salsa, and chicken with Serrano ham. For optimum nutrition, always serve these dishes with a large mixed-leaf salad or a low-carbohydrate vegetable dish.

stir-fried pork with dried shrimp

DRIED SHRIMP ARE A COMMON ingredient in many Asian cuisines. Their flavour is strong but, rather than overpowering a dish, they simply give a delicious savoury taste.

Serves 4
250g/9oz pork fillet (tenderloin)
30ml/2 tbsp vegetable oil
2 garlic cloves, finely chopped
45ml/3 tbsp dried shrimp
10ml/2 tsp dried shrimp paste or 5mm/¼in piece from block of shrimp paste
30ml/2 tbsp soy sauce
juice of 1 lime
15ml/1 tbsp palm sugar or light muscovado (brown) sugar
1 small fresh red or green chilli, seeded and finely chopped
4 pak choi (bok choy) or 450g/1lb spring greens (collards), shredded

1 Place the pork in the freezer for about 30 minutes, until firm. Remove from the freezer, then, using a sharp knife, cut it into thin slices.

2 Heat the oil in a wok or frying pan and cook the garlic until golden brown, but be careful not to let it burn. Add the pork and stir-fry for about 4 minutes, until just cooked through.

3 Add the dried shrimp, then stir in the shrimp paste with the soy sauce, lime juice and sugar. Add the chopped chilli and shredded pak choi or spring greens and toss over the heat until the vegetables are just beginning to wilt.

4 Transfer the stir-fry to warm individual bowls and serve immediately.

NUTRITION NOTES

Per portion:	
Energy	227kcal/949kJ
Protein	22.0g
Fat	12.6g
saturated fat	2.7g
Carbohydrate	6.6g
Fibre	3.7g
Calcium	241mg

COOK'S TIP

When using a wok, the oil should be very hot before you start cooking.

pork and pineapple coconut curry

THE HEAT OF THIS CURRY balances out its sweetness to make a smooth and fragrant dish. It takes very little time to cook, so is ideal for a quick supper or a midweek family meal.

Serves 4
400ml/14fl oz can or carton coconut milk
10ml/2 tsp Thai red curry paste
400g/14oz pork loin steaks, trimmed and thinly sliced
15ml/1 tbsp Thai fish sauce
5ml/1 tsp palm sugar or light muscovado (brown) sugar
15ml/1 tbsp tamarind juice, made by mixing tamarind paste with warm water
2 kaffir lime leaves, torn
½ medium pineapple, peeled and chopped
1 fresh red chilli, seeded and sliced

1 Pour the coconut milk into a bowl and let it settle, so that the cream rises to the surface. Scoop the cream into a measuring jug (cup). You should have about 250ml/8fl oz/1 cup. If necessary, add a little of the coconut milk.

2 Pour the coconut cream into a large pan and bring it to the boil.

3 Reduce the heat and simmer the coconut cream for about 10 minutes, until the cream separates, stirring frequently to prevent it from sticking to the base of the pan and scorching. Add the red curry paste and stir until well mixed. Cook, stirring occasionally, for about 4 minutes, until the paste is fragrant.

4 Add the sliced pork and stir in the fish sauce, sugar and tamarind juice. Cook, stirring constantly, for 1–2 minutes, until the sugar has dissolved and the pork is no longer pink.

5 Add the remaining coconut milk and the lime leaves. Bring to the boil, then stir in the pineapple. Reduce the heat and simmer for 3 minutes, or until the pork is cooked. Sprinkle over the chilli and serve.

NUTRITION NOTES

Per portion:	
Energy	223kcal/936kJ
Protein	22.0g
Fat	8.2g
saturated fat	3.0g
Carbohydrate	16.0g
Fibre	1.0g
Calcium	55mg

steak with warm tomato salsa

A REFRESHING, TANGY SALSA of tomatoes, spring onions and balsamic vinegar makes a colourful topping for chunky, pan-fried steaks. Serve with a mixed leaf salad and mustard dressing.

Serves 2

2 rump (round) steaks, about 2cm/¾in thick
3 large plum tomatoes
2 spring onions (scallions)
30ml/2 tbsp balsamic vinegar

NUTRITION NOTES

Per portion:	
Energy	502kcal/2105kJ
Protein	47g
Fat	33.5g
saturated fat	7.8g
Carbohydrate	3.0g
Fibre	1.4g
Calcium	35mg

1 Trim any fat from the steaks, then season on both sides. Heat a non-stick frying pan and cook the steaks for 3 minutes on each side for medium-rare. Cook for longer if you like your steak well-cooked.

2 Meanwhile, put the plum tomatoes in a heatproof bowl, cover with boiling water and leave for about 1–2 minutes, until the skins start to split. Drain and carefully peel the tomatoes, then halve them and scoop out the seeds with a spoon. Roughly chop the tomato flesh and thinly slice the spring onions.

3 Transfer the steaks to plates and keep warm. Add the vegetables, balsamic vinegar, 30ml/2 tbsp water and a little seasoning to the cooking juices in the pan and stir briefly until warm, scraping up any meat residue, which will add extra flavour. Spoon the warm tomato salsa over the steaks and serve immediately.

duck and sesame stir-fry

THIS RECIPE IS TRADITIONALLY intended for game birds, as farmed duck would usually have too much fat. Use wild duck if you can get it, or even partridge, pheasant or pigeon. If you do use farmed duck, you should remove the skin and fat layer.

Serves 4
250g/9oz wild duck breast portions
15ml/1 tbsp sesame oil
15ml/1 tbsp vegetable oil
4 garlic cloves, finely sliced
2.5ml/½ tsp dried chilli flakes
15ml/1 tbsp Thai fish sauce
15ml/1 tbsp light soy sauce
120ml/4fl oz/½ cup water
1 head broccoli, cut into small florets
coriander (cilantro) and 15ml/1 tbsp toasted sesame seeds, to garnish

VARIATIONS

Pak choi (bok choy) or Chinese flowering cabbage can be used instead of broccoli.

1 Cut the duck into bitesize pieces. Heat the oils in a wok or large, heavy frying pan and stir-fry the garlic over a medium heat until it is golden brown – do not let it burn. Add the duck pieces to the pan and stir-fry for a further 2 minutes, until the meat begins to brown.

2 Stir in the chilli flakes, fish sauce, soy sauce and water. Add the broccoli and continue to stir-fry for about 2 minutes, until the duck is just cooked through.

3 Serve on warmed plates, garnished with coriander and sesame seeds.

NUTRITION NOTES

Per portion:	
Energy	173kcal/721kJ
Protein	15.0g
Fat	10.9g
saturated fat	1.2g
Carbohydrate	3.2g
Fibre	1.8g
Calcium	57mg

chicken with serrano ham

LEAN CHICKEN IS AN IDEAL CHOICE for anyone following a low-carbohydrate diet. For a well-balanced meal serve with a large mixed green leaf and herb salad.

Serves 4

4 skinless, boneless chicken breast portions
4 slices Serrano ham
40g/1½oz/3 tbsp butter
30ml/2 tbsp chopped capers
30ml/2 tbsp fresh thyme leaves
1 large lemon, cut lengthways into 8 slices
a few small fresh thyme sprigs
salt and ground black pepper

COOK'S TIP

This dish is just as good with other thinly sliced cured ham, such as prosciutto, in place of the Serrano ham.

1 Preheat the oven to 200°C/400°F/Gas 6. Wrap each chicken breast portion loosely in clear film (plastic wrap) and beat with a rolling pin until flattened. Unwrap the chicken breast portions and arrange in a single layer in a large, shallow ovenproof dish. Top each piece of chicken with a slice of Serrano ham.

2 In a bowl, beat the butter with the capers, thyme and seasoning. Divide the butter into quarters and shape neat portions, then place on each ham-topped chicken breast portion. Arrange two lemon slices on the butter and sprinkle with thyme sprigs. Bake for 25 minutes, or until the chicken is cooked through.

3 Transfer the chicken portions to a warmed serving platter or four plates and spoon the piquant, buttery juices over the top. Serve immediately, removing the lemon slices first, if you prefer.

NUTRITION NOTES

Per portion:	
Energy	352kcal/1471kJ
Protein	52.7g
Fat	15.7g
saturated fat	8.5g
Carbohydrate	0g
Fibre	0g
Calcium	11mg

stir-fried chicken with basil and chilli

THIS QUICK AND EASY chicken dish is alive with the flavours of Thai cuisine. Thai basil, which is sometimes known as holy basil, has a unique, pungent flavour that is both spicy and sharp. Deep-frying the leaves adds another dimension to this dish.

Serves 6

45ml/3 tbsp vegetable oil
4 garlic cloves, thinly sliced
2–4 fresh red chillies, seeded and finely chopped
450g/1lb skinless, boneless chicken breast portions, cut into bitesize pieces
45ml/3 tbsp Thai fish sauce
10ml/2 tsp dark soy sauce
5ml/1 tsp granulated sugar
10–12 fresh Thai basil leaves
2 fresh red chillies, seeded and finely chopped, and about 20 deep-fried Thai basil leaves, to garnish

1 Heat the oil in a wok or frying pan. Add the garlic and chillies and stir-fry over a medium heat for 1–2 minutes until the garlic is golden. Take care not to let the garlic burn, otherwise it will taste bitter.

2 Add the pieces of chicken to the wok or pan, in batches if necessary, and stir-fry until the chicken changes colour.

3 Stir in the fish sauce, soy sauce and sugar. Continue to stir-fry the mixture for 3–4 minutes, or until the chicken is fully cooked and golden brown.

4 Stir in the fresh Thai basil leaves. Spoon the mixture on to a warm platter, or into individual dishes. Garnish with the chopped chillies and deep-fried Thai basil and serve immediately.

COOK'S TIP

To deep-fry Thai basil leaves, first make sure that the leaves are completely dry. Heat vegetable or groundnut (peanut) oil in a wok or deep-fryer to 190°C/375°F or until a cube of bread, added to the oil, browns in about 45 seconds. Add the leaves and deep-fry them briefly until they are crisp and translucent – this will take only about 30–40 seconds. Lift out the leaves using a slotted spoon and leave them to drain on kitchen paper before using.

NUTRITION NOTES

Per portion:	
Energy	271kcal/1130kJ
Protein	25.1g
Fat	16.3g
saturated fat	2.8g
Carbohydrate	5.0g
Fibre	0.2g
Calcium	25mg

fish and shellfish

FISH AND SHELLFISH CONTAIN essential vitamins and minerals, which are important in any diet. A huge variety of seafood is now available in supermarkets, and it is incredibly easy to cook. Among the healthiest and tastiest ways to prepare fish are to steam it or wrap a fillet in paper and bake in the oven – none of the nutrients will be lost if the fish is cooked like this. Prepare steamed lettuce-wrapped sole for a quick midweek meal, impress your guests with scallops with fennel and bacon or treat yourself to halibut with sauce vierge.

roasted cod with fresh tomato sauce

REALLY FRESH COD FILLETS have a sweet, delicate flavour and pure white flaky flesh. Served with an aromatic fresh tomato sauce, they make a delicious and nutritious meal.

NUTRITION NOTES

Per portion:	
Energy	354kcal/1492kJ
Protein	40.0g
Fat	20.3g
saturated fat	2.9g
Carbohydrate	3.0g
Fibre	1.3g
Calcium	48mg

Serves 4

- 350g/12oz ripe plum tomatoes
- 75ml/5 tbsp olive oil
- 2.5ml/½ tsp sugar
- 2 strips of pared orange rind
- 1 fresh thyme sprig
- 6 fresh basil leaves
- 900g/2lb fresh cod fillet, skin on
- salt and ground black pepper
- steamed green beans, to serve

1 Preheat the oven to 230°C/450°F/ Gas 8. Using a small, sharp knife, roughly chop the plum tomatoes, leaving their skins on, and set aside.

2 Heat 15ml/1 tbsp of the olive oil in a heavy pan, add the tomatoes, sugar, orange rind, thyme and basil, and simmer for 5 minutes, until the tomatoes are soft.

3 Press the tomato mixture through a fine sieve (strainer), discarding the solids that remain in the sieve. Pour into a small pan and heat gently.

4 Scale the cod fillet and cut on the diagonal into 4 pieces. Season well.

5 Heat the remaining oil in a heavy frying pan and fry the cod, skin side down, until the skin is crisp. Place the fish on a greased baking sheet, skin side up, and roast in the oven for 8–10 minutes, until cooked through. Serve the fish on top of the steamed green beans with the fresh tomato sauce.

VARIATIONS

Try haddock, pollock, coley or any other firm white fish instead of the cod.

steamed lettuce-wrapped sole

COOKING FOOD IN STEAM is extremely healthy as it helps to retain the nutrients that can be lost by other cooking methods. It also gives wonderfully succulent results.

Serves 4

2 large sole fillets, skinned
15ml/1 tbsp sesame seeds
15ml/1 tbsp sunflower or groundnut (peanut) oil
2.5cm/1in piece fresh root ginger, peeled and grated
3 garlic cloves, finely chopped
15ml/1 tbsp soy sauce or Thai fish sauce
juice of 1 lemon
2 spring onions (scallions), thinly sliced
8 large soft lettuce leaves
12 large live mussels, scrubbed and bearded
salt and ground black pepper
sesame oil, for drizzling (optional)

1 Cut the sole fillets in half lengthways. Season with salt and ground black pepper, then set aside.

2 Heat a dry frying pan until hot. Toast the sesame seeds lightly, until golden brown, then set aside.

3 Heat the sunflower or groundnut oil in the frying pan. Add the ginger and garlic and cook, stirring, until lightly coloured but not browned; stir in the soy sauce or Thai fish sauce, lemon juice and spring onions. Remove the pan from the heat and stir in the toasted sesame seeds.

4 Lay the pieces of fish on baking parchment, skinned side up; spread each evenly with the ginger mixture. Roll up each piece, starting at the tail end and place the rolls on a baking sheet.

5 Bring a pan of water, over which the steamer will fit, to the boil. Plunge the lettuce leaves into the boiling water and immediately lift them out. Lay them out flat on kitchen paper and pat dry.

6 Tightly wrap each sole parcel in two lettuce leaves, making sure they are very secure. Arrange the fish parcels in the steamer basket, cover and steam over simmering water for 8 minutes.

7 Add the mussels to the steamer and steam for 2–4 minutes, until they open. Discard any that remain closed. Put the parcels on four plates and garnish with the mussels. Serve drizzled with oil, if you like.

NUTRITION NOTES

Per portion:	
Energy	136kcal/568kJ
Protein	17.4g
Fat	7.1g
saturated fat	1.0g
Carbohydrate	0.6g
Fibre	0.3g
Calcium	47mg

grilled sea bass with fennel

THIS IS AN IMPRESSIVE DISH that is perfect for entertaining. Guests will never guess that this opulent dish is part of a successful healthy-eating, weight-loss diet.

Serves 8

1 sea bass, weighing 1.8–2kg/4–4½lb
60ml/4 tbsp olive oil
10–15ml/2–3 tsp fennel seeds
2 large fennel bulbs, trimmed and thinly sliced (reserve any fronds)
60ml/4 tbsp Pernod
salt and ground black pepper

NUTRITION NOTES

Per portion:	
Energy	308kcal/1287kJ
Protein	37.1g
Fat	15.3g
saturated fat	2.9g
Carbohydrate	3.2g
Fibre	0.9g
Calcium	44mg

1 With a sharp knife, make 3–4 deep cuts in both sides of the fish. Brush the fish with olive oil and season with salt and plenty of ground black pepper.

2 Sprinkle the fennel seeds in the cavity and into the cuts on both sides of the fish. Set aside while you cook the fennel.

3 Preheat the grill (broiler). Put the slices of fennel in a flameproof dish or on the grill rack and brush with a little olive oil. Cook for 4 minutes on each side until just tender. Transfer the fennel to a serving plate and set aside while you grill (broil) the fish.

4 Place the fish on the grill rack and position about 10–14cm/4–5½in away from the heat. Grill for 12 minutes on each side, brushing with oil occasionally during cooking.

5 Transfer the fish to the serving platter, placing it on top of the grilled fennel. Sprinkle over any reserved fennel fronds.

6 Heat the Pernod in a small pan, ignite it and pour it, flaming, over the fish. Serve immediately.

grilled halibut with sauce vierge

TOMATOES, CAPERS, ANCHOVIES, herbs and fresh lemon make a vibrant sauce that is perfect for halibut, but it is so versatile that it will suit any thick white fish fillets.

Serves 4
105ml/7 tbsp olive oil
2.5ml/½ tsp fennel seeds
2.5ml/½ tsp celery seeds
5ml/1 tsp mixed peppercorns
5ml/1 tsp fresh thyme leaves, chopped
5ml/1 tsp fresh rosemary leaves, chopped
5ml/1 tsp fresh oregano or marjoram leaves, chopped
675–800g/1½–1¾lb middle cut of halibut, about 3cm/1¼in thick, cut into four pieces
coarse sea salt
shredded lettuce and lemon wedges, to serve

For the sauce
2 tomatoes
105ml/7 tbsp extra virgin olive oil
juice of 1 lemon
1 garlic clove, finely chopped
5ml/1 tsp small capers
2 drained canned anchovy fillets, chopped
5ml/1 tsp chopped fresh chives
15ml/1 tbsp shredded fresh basil leaves
15ml/1 tbsp chopped fresh chervil

1 For the sauce, plunge the tomatoes into boiling water for about 30 seconds or until the skins split, then refresh them in cold water. Peel off the skins, remove the seeds with a teaspoon and finely dice the flesh. Set aside.

2 Heat a ridged griddle or preheat the grill (broiler) to high. Brush the griddle or grill pan with a little of the olive oil.

VARIATIONS

Try turbot, brill or John Dory, or even humbler fish, such as cod or haddock, with this tangy sauce.

3 Meanwhile, mix the fennel and celery seeds with the peppercorns in a mortar. Crush with a pestle, and then stir in sea salt to taste. Spoon the mixture into a large, flat dish and stir in the herbs and the remaining olive oil.

NUTRITION NOTES

Per portion:	
Energy	653kcal/2742kJ
Protein	32.5g
Fat	57.5g
saturated fat	8.0g
Carbohydrate	1.3g
Fibre	0.4g
Calcium	47mg

4 Add the halibut pieces to the olive oil and herb mixture, turning them to coat thoroughly, then arrange them on the oiled griddle or grill pan with the dark skin uppermost. Cook for approximately 7 minutes, turning once, or until the fish is completely cooked through and the skin is nicely browned.

5 Combine all the sauce ingredients, except for the fresh herbs, in a pan and heat gently until warm but not hot. Gradually stir in the chives, basil leaves and fresh chervil.

6 Place the halibut on four plates and spoon the sauce over the fish. Serve with the lettuce and lemon wedges.

warm swordfish and peppery salad

ROBUST SWORDFISH teamed with peppery salad makes a healthy meal that's perfect for any occasion, whether it's part of a low-carbohydrate eating plan or a sophisticated dinner.

Serves 4

4 swordfish steaks, 150g/5oz each
75ml/5 tbsp extra virgin olive oil
juice of 1 lemon
30ml/2 tbsp finely chopped parsley
115g/4oz rocket (arugula) leaves
115g/4oz Pecorino cheese
salt and ground black pepper

1 Lay the swordfish steaks in a shallow dish. In a small jug (pitcher) or bowl, mix about 60ml/4 tbsp of the olive oil with the lemon juice. Pour the mixture over the fish. Season with salt and ground black pepper, sprinkle on the finely chopped parsley and turn the fish to coat well. Cover with clear film (plastic wrap) and leave to marinate for at least 10 minutes.

2 Heat a ridged griddle pan or the grill (broiler) until very hot. Remove the fish steaks from the marinade and pat dry with kitchen paper.

3 Place the fish steaks in the griddle pan or under the grill (broiler) and cook for 2 minutes on each side until the swordfish is opaque and just cooked through.

4 Meanwhile, remove the stems from the rocket leaves and put the leaves in a large bowl. Season with salt and pepper. Drizzle over the remaining olive oil and toss well to combine. Shave the Pecorino cheese over the top of the salad leaves.

5 Place the swordfish steaks on four individual plates and arrange a little pile of salad on each steak. Serve immediately, while still warm.

NUTRITION NOTES

Per portion:	
Energy	451kcal/1885kJ
Protein	43.6g
Fat	30.5g
saturated fat	9.5g
Carbohydrate	0.5g
Fibre	0.6g
Calcium	400mg

fresh tuna and tomato stew

THIS DELICIOUSLY SIMPLE Italian recipe relies on good basic ingredients: fresh fish, ripe tomatoes and mixed herbs. Serve with a crisp green salad for a healthy, satisfying meal.

Serves 4
12 baby (pearl) onions, peeled
900g/2lb ripe tomatoes
675g/1½lb tuna
45ml/3 tbsp olive oil
2 garlic cloves, crushed
45ml/3 tbsp chopped fresh herbs
2 bay leaves
2.5ml/½ tsp caster (superfine) sugar
30ml/2 tbsp sun-dried tomato purée (paste)
150ml/¼ pint/⅔ cup dry white wine
salt and ground black pepper
baby courgettes (zucchini) and fresh herbs, to garnish

1 Leave the onions whole and cook in a pan of boiling water for 4–5 minutes until softened. Drain. Plunge the tomatoes into boiling water for 30 seconds, then refresh in cold water. Peel and chop roughly.

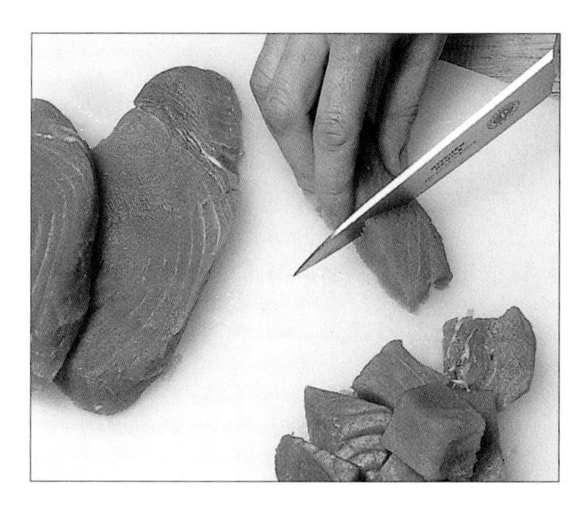

2 Cut the tuna into 2.5cm/1in chunks. Heat the oil in a large frying or sauté pan and quickly fry the tuna until the surface has browned. Remove with a slotted spoon and set aside.

VARIATION

Two large mackerel could be used instead of tuna. Lay the whole fish over the sauce and cook, covered with a lid, until the mackerel is cooked through.

3 Stir in the garlic, tomatoes, chopped herbs, bay leaves, sugar, tomato purée and white wine, and bring to the boil, breaking up the tomatoes with a wooden spoon. Add the onions.

4 Reduce the heat and simmer the sauce gently for 5 minutes. Return the fish to the pan and cook for a further 5 minutes. Season, and serve hot, garnished with baby courgettes and fresh herbs.

NUTRITION NOTES

Per portion:	
Energy	381kcal/1589kJ
Protein	42.7g
Fat	19.6g
saturated fat	3.8g
Carbohydrate	13.0g
Fibre	4.2g
Calcium	77mg

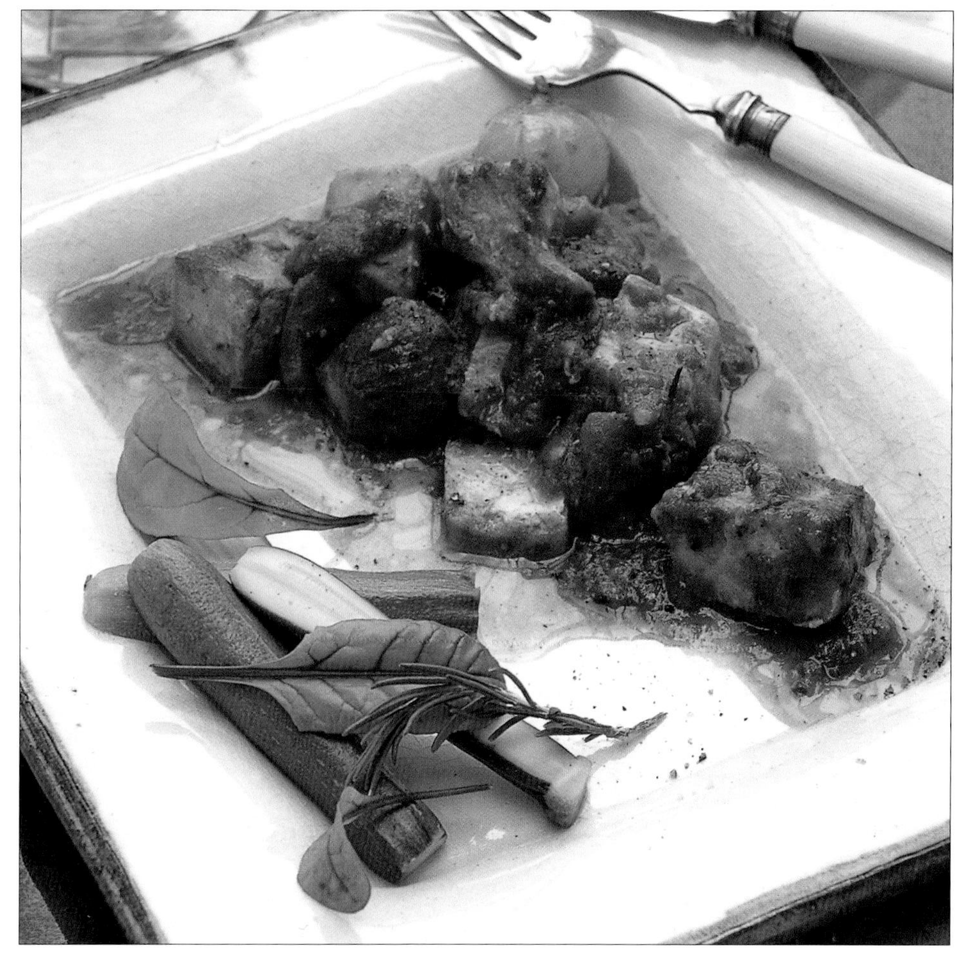

scallops with fennel and bacon

THIS IMPRESSIVE DISH IS A DELICIOUS combination of succulent scallops and crispy bacon, served on a bed of tender fennel and melting mascarpone cheese – irresistible.

Serves 2

2 small fennel bulbs
130g/4½oz/generous ½ cup mascarpone cheese
8 large scallops, shelled
75g/3oz thin smoked streaky (fatty) bacon rashers (strips)

NUTRITION NOTES

Per portion:	
Energy	658kcal/2744kJ
Protein	57.5g
Fat	46.2g
saturated fat	25.5g
Carbohydrate	3.3g
Fibre	2.2g
Calcium	287mg

1 Trim, halve and slice the fennel bulbs thinly, chopping any feathery tops and reserving them to be used as a garnish. Bring a large pan of water to the boil and blanch the fennel slices for about 3 minutes, or until soft and tender. Drain well and set aside.

2 Preheat the grill (broiler) to medium. Place the fennel in a shallow flameproof dish and season. Dot with the mascarpone and grill (broil) for about 5 minutes, until the cheese has melted and the fennel is lightly browned.

3 Meanwhile, pat the scallops dry with kitchen paper. Cook the bacon in a frying pan, until crisp and golden, turning once. Drain and keep warm. Fry the scallops in the bacon fat for 1–2 minutes on each side, until cooked through.

4 Transfer the fennel to serving plates and crumble or snip the bacon into bitesize pieces over the top. Pile the scallops on the bacon and sprinkle with any reserved fennel tops.

pan-steamed mussels with thai herbs

LIKE SO MANY Thai dishes, these mussels are extremely easy to prepare and ready in minutes. The lemon grass stalks and kaffir lime leaves add a refreshing tang to the fresh mussels.

Serves 4

- 1kg/2¼lb fresh mussels
- 2 lemon grass stalks, finely chopped
- 4 shallots, chopped
- 4 kaffir lime leaves, coarsely torn
- 2 fresh red chillies, sliced
- 15ml/1 tbsp Thai fish sauce (*nam pla*)
- 30ml/2 tbsp fresh lime juice
- thinly sliced spring onions (scallions), to garnish

1 Clean the mussels by pulling off the beards and scrubbing the shells well. Discard any mussels that are broken or which are open and do not close when tapped sharply.

2 Place the mussels in a large, heavy pan and add the lemon grass, shallots, kaffir lime leaves, chillies, fish sauce and lime juice. Mix well. Cover the pan tightly and steam the mussels over a high heat, shaking the pan occasionally, for 5–7 minutes, until the shells have opened.

COOK'S TIP

Mussels are available all year round and are relatively cheap. Buy slightly more than you think you will need to allow for wastage. Store fresh mussels in the refrigerator and eat within one day of purchase.

3 Using a slotted spoon, transfer the cooked mussels to a warmed serving dish or individual bowls. Discard any mussels that have failed to open.

4 Garnish the mussels with the thinly sliced spring onions. Serve immediately in deep bowls, with small side plates for the empty shells.

NUTRITION NOTES

Per portion:	
Energy	83kcal/353kJ
Protein	14.0g
Fat	1.8g
saturated fat	0.3g
Carbohydrate	2.8g
Fibre	0.4g
Calcium	25mg

vegetarian dishes

IT IS IMPORTANT TO make sure you eat enough protein if you are a vegetarian on a low-carbohydrate diet. Nutritious meals based around lentils, beans, nuts, eggs and tofu are essential, and make sure you eat plenty of fresh green vegetables to obtain the recommended daily allowance of essential vitamins and minerals. Substantial and filling meals include lemony okra and tomato tagine or tofu and green bean red curry. For a delicious light lunch, try aromatic Chinese omelette parcels.

chinese omelette parcels

STIR-FRIED FRESH VEGETABLES cooked in a tasty black bean sauce make a really unusual yet remarkably good omelette filling, for a quick low-carb lunch.

Serves 4

130g/4½oz broccoli, cut into small florets
30ml/2 tbsp groundnut (peanut) oil
1cm/½in piece of fresh root ginger, finely grated
1 large garlic clove, crushed
2 red chillies, seeded and thinly sliced
4 spring onions (scallions), sliced diagonally
175g/6oz/3 cups pak choi (bok choy), shredded
50g/2oz/2 cups fresh coriander (cilantro) leaves, plus extra to garnish
115g/4oz/2 cups beansprouts
45ml/3 tbsp black bean sauce
4 eggs
salt and ground black pepper

1 Blanch the broccoli in salted, boiling water for 2 minutes, drain well, then refresh under cold running water.

2 Meanwhile, heat 15ml/1 tbsp oil in a frying pan or wok. Add the ginger, garlic and half the chilli and stir-fry for 1 minute. Add the spring onions, broccoli and pak choi and stir-fry for 2 minutes, tossing the vegetables to prevent them sticking.

3 Chop three-quarters of the coriander and add to the frying pan or wok. Add the beansprouts and stir-fry for 1 minute, then add the black bean sauce and heat through for 1 minute more. Remove the pan from the heat and keep warm.

4 Beat the eggs lightly and season well with salt and ground black pepper. Heat a little of the remaining groundnut oil in a small frying pan and add a quarter of the beaten egg. Swirl the egg until it covers the base of the pan, then sprinkle over a quarter of the reserved coriander leaves. Cook until set, then carefully turn out on to a plate and keep warm in the oven while you make three more omelettes, adding a little more oil when necessary.

5 Spoon the vegetable stir-fry on to the omelettes and roll up. Cut in half crossways and serve garnished with coriander leaves and chilli.

COOK'S TIP

Black bean sauce is available in jars or cans from most large supermarkets.

NUTRITION NOTES

Per portion:	
Energy	184kcal/767kJ
Protein	9.7g
Fat	13.1g
saturated fat	3.1g
Carbohydrate	5.5g
Fibre	3.1g
Calcium	127mg

lemony okra and tomato tagine

IN THIS SPICY VEGETABLE DISH, the heat of the chilli is offset by the refreshing flavour of lemon juice. Based on a Moroccan recipe, this is ideal as a light main course with a side salad.

Serves 4
350g/12oz okra
5–6 tomatoes
2 small onions
2 garlic cloves, crushed
1 fresh green chilli, seeded
5ml/1 tsp paprika
small handful of fresh coriander (cilantro), plus extra to garnish
30ml/2 tbsp sunflower oil
juice of 1 lemon

1 Trim the okra and then cut them into 1cm/½in lengths. Set aside.

2 Cut the tomatoes in half and scoop out the seeds with a teaspoon. Chop the fleah coarsely and set aside.

3 Coarsely chop one of the onions and place it in a food processor or blender with the crushed garlic, green chilli, paprika, fresh coriander and 60ml/4 tbsp water. Process to a smooth paste.

4 Heat the sunflower oil in a large pan. Thinly slice the second onion and cook gently in the oil for about 5–6 minutes, or until soft and a golden brown colour. Transfer the cooked onion slices to a plate with a slotted spoon.

5 Reduce the heat and pour in the onion and coriander mixture. Cook for 1–2 minutes, stirring frequently, and then add the okra pieces, chopped tomatoes, lemon juice and about 120ml/4fl oz/½ cup water.

6 Stir well to mix, cover tightly, and simmer gently over a low heat for about 15 minutes, or until the okra is tender.

7 Transfer to a large warmed serving dish, sprinkle with the fried onion rings, garnish with fresh coriander and serve immediately.

NUTRITION NOTES

Per portion:	
Energy	106kcal/438kJ
Protein	2.9g
Fat	7.5g
saturated fat	1.0g
Carbohydrate	6.5g
Fibre	2.9g
Calcium	83mg

tofu and green bean red curry

THIS IS ONE OF THOSE versatile recipes that should be in every cook's repertoire. This version uses green beans, but other types of vegetable work equally well.

Serves 4

600ml/1 pint/2½ cups canned coconut milk
15ml/1 tbsp Thai red curry paste
45ml/3 tbsp Thai fish sauce (*nam pla*)
10ml/2 tsp palm sugar or light muscovado (brown) sugar
225g/8oz/3¼ cups button (white) mushrooms
115g/4oz/scant 1 cup green beans, trimmed
175g/6oz firm tofu, rinsed, drained and cut in 2cm/¾in cubes
4 kaffir lime leaves, torn
2 fresh red chillies, seeded and sliced
fresh coriander (cilantro) leaves, to garnish

1 Pour about one-third of the coconut milk into a wok or pan. Cook gently until it starts to separate and an oily sheen appears on the surface.

2 Add the red curry paste, fish sauce and sugar to the coconut milk. Mix thoroughly, then add the mushrooms. Stir and cook for 1 minute.

3 Stir in the remaining coconut milk. Bring back to the boil, then add the green beans and tofu cubes. Simmer gently for 4–5 minutes more.

4 Stir in the kaffir lime leaves and sliced red chillies. Spoon the curry into a serving dish, garnish with the coriander leaves and serve immediately.

NUTRITION NOTES

Per portion:	
Energy	105kcal/438kJ
Protein	6.0g
Fat	3.1g
saturated fat	0.6g
Carbohydrate	12.8g
Fibre	2.4g
Calcium	75mg

COOK'S TIP

Fresh tofu can be kept in plenty of water in the refrigerator for up to three days, if the water is changed daily.

balti stir-fried vegetables with cashews

THIS VERSATILE STIR-FRY recipe will accommodate most combinations of vegetables so feel free to experiment. The cashew nuts add a delicious crunch to the dish.

Serves 4
2 carrots
1 red (bell) pepper, seeded
1 green (bell) pepper, seeded
2 courgettes (zucchini)
115g/4oz green beans, halved
1 bunch of spring onions (scallions)
15ml/1 tbsp extra virgin olive oil
4–6 curry leaves
2.5ml/½ tsp cumin seeds
4 dried red chillies
10–12 cashew nuts
5ml/1 tsp salt
30ml/2 tbsp lemon juice
fresh mint leaves, to garnish

1 Cut the carrots, peppers and courgettes into matchsticks, halve the beans and chop the spring onions. Set aside.

2 Heat the oil in a wok and stir-fry the curry leaves, cumin seeds and dried chillies for 1 minute.

3 Add the vegetables and nuts and toss them over the heat for 3–4 minutes. Add the salt and lemon juice and stir-fry for about 2 minutes more, until the vegetables are crisp-tender.

4 Transfer to a warm dish and serve garnished with mint leaves.

COOK'S TIP

When making stir-fries, it is a good idea to use a non-stick wok to minimize the amount of oil needed. However, it cannot be heated to the same high temperature as a conventional wok.

NUTRITION NOTES

Per portion:	
Energy	100kcal/420kJ
Protein	3.1g
Fat	5.7g
saturated fat	0.8g
Carbohydrate	9.1g
Fibre	3.2g
Calcium	92mg

side dishes

EATING PLENTY OF VEGETABLES is an essential part of any healthy diet, and having a good proportion of them raw, as salads, ensures they keep the maximum nutritional value. All vegetables contain carbohydrate but some contain far more than others and some are absorbed more gradually, which helps to maintain steady blood sugar levels. Starchy vegetables, such as potatoes and yams, are strictly off limits, but any other vegetables are good choices for side dishes or salads. Try crisp pak choi with lime dressing or a nutritious mixed green leaf and herb salad.

mexican-style green peas

THIS DISH, USING FRESH PEAS, is a delicious accompaniment to any meal. Use vine tomatoes and organic peas if possible.

Serves 4
2 tomatoes
15ml/1 tbsp olive oil
2 garlic cloves, halved
1 medium onion, halved and thinly sliced
400g/14oz/scant 3 cups shelled fresh peas
30ml/2 tbsp water
salt and ground black pepper
fresh chives, to garnish

1 Plunge the tomatoes into a bowl of boiling water. Leave them for 3 minutes, until the skins split, then drain, plunge into cold water and peel the skins off. Cut the tomatoes in half and squeeze out the seeds. Chop the flesh into 1cm/½in dice.

2 Heat the oil in a pan and cook the garlic until golden. Scoop it out with a slotted spoon and discard.

3 Add the onion to the pan and fry until transparent. Add the tomatoes and peas.

4 Pour over the water, lower the heat and cover the pan tightly. Cook for about 10 minutes, until the peas are cooked. Season with plenty of salt and pepper, transfer the mixture to a heated dish and serve, garnished with fresh chives.

NUTRITION NOTES

Per portion:	
Energy	113kcal/476kJ
Protein	6.4g
Fat	4.2g
saturated fat	0.7g
Carbohydrate	13.3g
Fibre	5.9g
Calcium	27mg

mushrooms with chipotle chillies

CHIPOTLE CHILLIES are jalapeños that have been smoke-dried. They are the perfect foil for the mushrooms in this simple salad.

Serves 6
2 chipotle chillies
450g/1lb/6 cups button (white) mushrooms
60ml/4 tbsp vegetable oil
1 onion, finely chopped
2 garlic cloves, crushed or chopped
fresh coriander (cilantro), to garnish

NUTRITION NOTES

Per portion:	
Energy	109kcal/455kJ
Protein	1.8g
Fat	10.5g
saturated fat	1.1g
Carbohydrate	1.6g
Fibre	2.1g
Calcium	11mg

1 Soak the dried chillies in a bowl of hot water for about 10 minutes. Drain, cut off the stalks, then slit the chillies and scrape out the seeds. Chop the flesh finely.

2 Trim the mushrooms, clean them and cut them in half, if large.

3 Heat the oil in a large frying pan. Add the onion, garlic, chillies and mushrooms and stir until evenly coated in the oil. Fry for 6–8 minutes, until the onion is tender. Transfer to a warmed dish. Chop some of the coriander, leaving some whole leaves, and use to garnish. Serve hot.

mixed green leaf and herb salad

THIS FLAVOURFUL SALAD makes an ideal side dish that goes well with meat and fish. You could turn it into a more substantial dish for a light lunch by trying one of the variations.

Serves 4

15g/½oz/½ cup mixed fresh herbs, such as chervil, tarragon (use sparingly), dill, basil, marjoram (use sparingly), flat leaf parsley, mint, sorrel, fennel and coriander (cilantro)

350g/12oz mixed salad leaves, such as rocket (arugula), radicchio, chicory (Belgian endive), watercress, frisée, baby spinach, oakleaf lettuce and dandelion

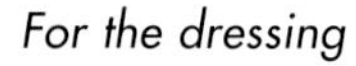

For the dressing

50ml/2fl oz/¼ cup extra virgin olive oil

15ml/1 tbsp cider vinegar

salt and ground black pepper

1 Wash and dry the herbs and salad leaves in a salad spinner, or use two clean, dry dishtowels to pat them dry.

2 To make the dressing, blend together the olive oil and cider vinegar in a small bowl and season with salt and ground black pepper to taste.

3 Place the mixed herbs and salad leaves in a large salad bowl. Just before serving, pour over the dressing and toss thoroughly to mix well, using your hands. Serve immediately.

VARIATIONS

To make a more substantial salad for a light lunch or supper, try adding some of the following ingredients:

- Baby broad (fava) beans, cooked, sliced artichoke hearts and quartered hard-boiled eggs
- Cooked chickpeas, asparagus tips and pitted green olives.

NUTRITION NOTES

Per portion:	
Energy	111kcal/463kJ
Protein	0.7g
Fat	11.4g
saturated fat	1.7g
Carbohydrate	1.5g
Fibre	0.8g
Calcium	25mg

pak choi with lime dressing

THE COCONUT DRESSING for this dish is traditionally made using Thai fish sauce, but mushroom sauce is a suitable vegetarian alternative. Beware, this is a fiery dish!

Serves 4
30ml/2 tbsp oil
3 fresh red chillies, cut into thin strips
4 garlic cloves, thinly sliced
6 spring onions (scallions), sliced diagonally
2 pak choi (bok choy), shredded
15ml/1 tbsp crushed peanuts

For the dressing
30ml/2 tbsp fresh lime juice
15–30ml/1–2 tbsp Thai fish sauce (*nam pla*)
250ml/8fl oz/1 cup coconut milk

1 Make the dressing. Put the lime juice and fish sauce in a bowl and mix well, then gradually whisk in the coconut milk until thoroughly combined.

2 Heat the oil in a wok and stir-fry the chillies for 2–3 minutes, until crisp. Transfer to a plate using a slotted spoon. Add the garlic to the wok and stir-fry for 30–60 seconds, until golden brown. Transfer to the plate.

3 Stir-fry the white parts of the spring onions for about 2–3 minutes, then add the green parts and stir-fry for 1 minute more. Transfer to the plate.

4 Bring a large pan of lightly salted water to the boil and add the pak choi. Stir twice, then drain immediately.

5 Place the pak choi in a large bowl, add the dressing and toss to mix. Spoon into a large serving bowl and sprinkle with the crushed peanuts and the stir-fried chilli mixture. Serve warm or cold.

NUTRITION NOTES

Per portion:	
Energy	134kcal/564kJ
Protein	3.1g
Fat	9.6g
saturated fat	1.4g
Carbohydrate	8.8g
Fibre	1.8g
Calcium	81mg

desserts

FOR THOSE WITH A SWEET TOOTH, sticking to a low-carbohydrate diet and avoiding all things sweet and indulgent may sound impossible. However, there are plenty of sweet treats that won't ruin the diet if they are eaten occasionally. This chapter offers inspiration in creating delicious desserts that are relatively low in carbohydrate and will make the perfect end to a special meal. Round off a summer barbecue with fresh fruit salad or, for something more filling, try a juicy, fruit-filled soufflé omelette.

fresh fruit salad

A LIGHT AND REFRESHING fruit salad makes a healthy and nutritious end to a low-carbohydrate meal. The natural fruit sugars are kinder to the body than refined sugars.

Serves 6
2 peaches
2 oranges
2 eating apples
16–20 strawberries
30ml/2 tbsp lemon juice
15–30ml/1–2 tbsp orange flower water
a few fresh mint leaves, to decorate

1 Place the peaches in a bowl and pour over boiling water. Leave to stand for 1 minute, then lift out with a slotted spoon, peel, stone (pit) and cut the flesh into thick slices.

2 Peel the oranges with a sharp knife, removing all the white pith, and segment them, catching any juice in a bowl.

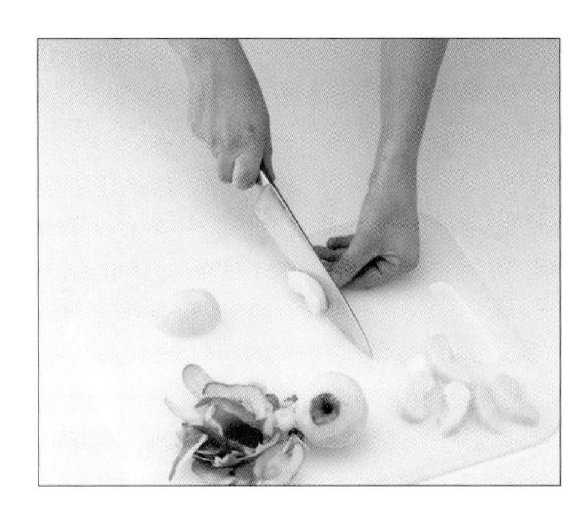

3 Peel and core the apples and cut into thin slices. Using the point of a knife, hull the strawberries and halve or quarter the fruits if they are large. Place all the prepared fruit in a large serving bowl.

NUTRITION NOTES

Per portion:	
Energy	39kcal/163kJ
Protein	0.8g
Fat	0.1g
saturated fat	0g
Carbohydrate	9.3g
Fibre	1.6g
Calcium	10mg

4 Blend together the lemon juice, orange flower water and any reserved orange juice. Pour the fruit juice mixture over the salad and toss lightly. Serve decorated with a few fresh mint leaves.

fruit-filled soufflé omelette

A LIGHT AND FLUFFY soufflé omelette filled with fresh, juicy strawberries is a decadent and indulgent treat that is naturally low in carbohydrate.

Serves 3

75g/3oz/¾ cup strawberries, hulled
3 eggs, separated
30ml/2 tbsp caster (superfine) sugar
45ml/3 tbsp double (heavy) cream, whipped
a few drops of vanilla essence (extract)
25g/1oz/2 tbsp butter

1 Hull the strawberries and cut them in half. Set aside. In a bowl, beat the egg yolks and sugar until pale and fluffy, then fold in the cream and vanilla essence. Whisk the egg whites in a very large, grease-free bowl until stiff, then carefully fold into the yolks.

2 Melt the butter in an omelette pan. When sizzling, pour in the egg mixture and cook until set, shaking occasionally. Spoon on the strawberries and, tilting the pan, slide the omelette so that it folds over.

3 Carefully slide the omelette on to a warm serving plate. Cut the omelette into three pieces, then transfer to three warmed plates and serve immediately.

VARIATION

Use any type of soft, non-starchy fruit in place of the strawberries. Slices of peach, fresh berries or a combination of several fruits will all work well.

NUTRITION NOTES

Per portion:	
Energy	205kcal/854kJ
Protein	7.6g
Fat	14.2g
saturated fat	6.8g
Carbohydrate	12.5g
Fibre	0.3g
Calcium	51mg

frozen melon

FREEZING SORBET in hollowed-out fruit, which is then cut into wedges, is an excellent idea. The refreshing flavour makes this dessert irresistible on a hot summer's day.

Serves 6

50g/2oz/¼ cup caster (superfine) sugar
30ml/2 tbsp clear honey
15ml/1 tbsp lemon juice
60ml/4 tbsp water
1 medium cantaloupe melon or Charentais melon, about 1kg/2¼lb
crushed ice, cucumber slices and borage flowers, to decorate

1 Put the sugar, honey, lemon juice and water in a heavy pan and heat gently until the sugar dissolves. Bring to the boil, and boil for 1 minute, without stirring, to make a syrup. Leave to cool.

2 Cut the melon in half and discard the seeds. Carefully scoop out the flesh using a metal spoon or melon baller and place in a food processor, taking care to keep the halved shells intact.

3 Process the melon flesh until very smooth, then transfer to a large mixing bowl. Stir in the cooled sugar syrup and chill until very cold. Invert the melon shells and leave them to drain on kitchen paper for a few minutes, then transfer them to the freezer while making the sorbet.

4 If making by hand, pour the mixture into a plastic container and freeze for about 3–4 hours, beating twice with a fork or a whisk, or processing in a food processor, to break up the ice crystals and produce a smoother texture. If using an ice cream maker, churn the melon mixture until the sorbet holds its shape.

5 Remove the melon shells from the freezer, pack the frozen sorbet tightly into the melon shells and level the surface with a sharp knife.

6 Use a dessertspoon to scoop out the centre of each filled melon shell to simulate the seed cavity, then freeze the prepared fruit overnight until firm.

7 To serve, use a large knife to cut each melon half into three large wedges. Serve on a bed of crushed ice either on a large platter or individual plates, and decorate with the cucumber slices and borage flowers.

COOK'S TIP

If the melon sorbet is too firm to cut when taken straight from the freezer, let it soften in the refrigerator for 10–20 minutes. Take care when slicing the frozen melon into wedges. A serrated kitchen knife is easier to work with.

NUTRITION NOTES

Per portion:	
Energy	87kcal/364kJ
Protein	1.7g
Fat	0g
saturated fat	0g
Carbohydrate	21.3g
Fibre	1.7g
Calcium	32mg

checking carbohydrate content

THE FOLLOWING list shows the glycaemic index (GI) and carbohydrate content of many common foods. On a low-carbohydrate diet, try to choose foods with a low GI (55 or less), which indicates that they are absorbed slowly into the bloodstream, as well as a low carbohydrate content.

FOOD	PORTION	GI	CARB
apple	1 fruit	38	18g
apple juice	250ml	40	33g
apricots	3 fruits	57	7g
dried	5 (40g)	31	15g
bacon	2 rashers	0	0g
bagel, white	1	72	35g
baked beans	120g	48	13g
banana			
ripe	1 fruit	55	32g
unripe	1 fruit	30	11g
barley	80g	25	17g
beef	120g	0	0g
beetroot (beet)	60g	64	5g
biscuits (cookies)			
arrowroot	3 biscuits	63	15g
Digestives (graham crackers)	2 biscuits	59	21g
morning coffee	3 biscuits	79	14g
Rich Tea	2 biscuits	55	14g
shortbread	2 biscuits	64	19g
black beans	120g	43	16g
black-eyed beans (peas)	120g	42	24g
bread			
baguette	30g	95	15g
bread roll, soft	45g	69	21g
chapati (Baisen)	1	27	38g
chapati (Bajra)	1	57	42g
fruit loaf	1 slice	47	18g
hamburger bun	50g	61	24g
oat bran and honey loaf with barley (Burgen)	2 slices	31	21g
pitta bread	1 piece	57	38g
pumpernickel	1 slice	41	35g
rye bread	1 slice	65	23g
white	1 slice	70	15g
white (gluten-free)	2 slices	90	37g
wholemeal (whole-wheat)	1 slice	69	14g
breadfruit	120g	68	17g
breakfast cereals			
All-Bran	40g	42	22g
Bran Buds	40g	58	17g
Cheerios	30g	74	20g
Cocopops	30g	77	29g
Cornflakes	30g	84	26g
Golden Grahams	30g	71	30g
muesli (granola)	60g	56	32g
porridge (oatmeal)	245g	42	24g
puffed wheat	30g	80	22g
Rice Krispies	30g	82	27g
Shredded Wheat	2 biscuits	67	30g
Special K	30g	54	24g
Sultana Bran	30g	52	28g
Sustain	30g	68	30g
Weetabix	2 biscuits	74	28g
broad (fava) beans	80g	79	9g
buckwheat	80g	54	57g
bulgur wheat	120g	48	22g
butter (lima) beans	70g	31	13g
cakes			
angel food	60g	47	50g
banana	1 slice	47	46g
carrot	85g	62	45g
sponge	120g	33	22g
carrots	60g	71	3g
cheese	120g	0	0g
cherries	100g	22	12g
chicken	120g	0	0g
chickpeas, canned	4tbsp	31	22g
chocolate, milk	30g	49	19g
Mars bar	medium bar	68	43g
Snickers	medium bar	41	29g
corn	85g	54	16g
corn chips	50g	42	33g
cornmeal	40g	68	30g
couscous	120g	65	28g
crispbreads (rye)	2	69	14g
croissant	1	67	27g
crumpet	1	69	22g
custard	175g	43	24g
dhal	1tbsp	54	8g
dates, dried	3	103	29g
doughnut	40g	76	16g
eggs	120g	0	0g
fish	120g	0	0g
fish fingers (breaded fish sticks)	5 fingers	38	24g
flour tortilla	1 wrap	38	38g
fructose	1tsp (5g)	23	5g

glucose	1tsp (5g)	100	5g
gnocchi	145g	68	71g
grapefruit	½ fruit	25	5g
grapefruit juice	250ml	48	16g
grapes	100g	46	15g
haricot (navy)			
beans	90g	38	11g
honey	15ml	58	16g
ice cream	2 scoops	61	10g
low fat	50g	50	12g
jam (strawberry)	2 tsp	51	7g
kidney beans	4 tbsp	27	20g
kiwi fruit	1 fruit	52	8g
lamb	120g	0	0g
lentils	95g	30	16g
Lucozade	250ml	95	40g
lychees, canned	7 fruits	79	16g
mango	1 small fruit	55	19g
marmalade	30g	48	20g
melba toast	4 toasts	70	21g
milk,			
full-fat (whole)	250ml	27	12g
skimmed	250ml	32	13g
soya	200ml	31	18g
muesli (granola) bar	1 bar (33g)	61	20g
muffin			
apple	80g	10	44g
blueberry	1 bun	59	31g
noodles	85g	46	55g
nuts (see peanuts)			
oatcakes (Scottish)	1 triangle	57	10g
orange	1 fruit	44	10g
juice	250ml	46	21g
squash (drink)	40ml	66	12g
papaya	½ fruit	58	14g
parsnips	75g	97	8g

pasta			
fettucini	150g	32	40g
linguine	150g	43	39g
macaroni	140g	45	35g
macaroni and			
cheese (boxed)	250g	64	38g
ravioli	250g	39	45g
spaghetti, white	180g	41	56g
spaghetti wholemeal			
(whole-wheat)	180g	41	56g
tortellini	180g	50	21g
tortellini			
(cheese-filled)	320g	50	49g
pastry	65g	59	25g
peaches	1 fruit	42	7g
canned	120g	30	12g
peanuts	75g	14	11g
chocolate	47g	33	17g
pear	1 fruit	38	21g
peas	80g	48	5g
dried marrowfat	60g	39	12g
pineapple	2 slices	66	10g
juice	150ml	46	20g
pinto beans,			
cooked	60g	39	9g
pizza	2 slices	60	57g
plums	3 fruits	39	7g
popcorn	20g	55	10g
pork	120g	0	0g
potatoes			
baked	120g	85	14g
boiled	120g	56	16g
canned	100g	61	13g
crisps (US chips)	50g	54	24g
French fries	120g	75	49g
mashed	120g	70	16g

pretzels	50g	83	22g
pumpkin	85g	75	6g
raisins	40g	64	28g
rice			
brown	25g	55	20g
risotto	150g	69	53g
white basmati	180g	58	50g
white glutinous	175g	98	37g
wild	50g	54	39g
rice cakes	2	82	21g
romano beans,			
cooked	60g	46	8g
rye	25g	34	16g
sausages	2	28	12g
semolina	25g	55	19g
shellfish	120g	0	0g
soup			
green pea	200ml	66	19g
lentil	200ml	44	24g
split pea	200ml	60	28g
tomato	200ml	38	14g
soya beans	100g	14	12g
split peas	60g	32	13g
swede (rutabaga),			
boiled	60g	72	2g
sweet potato	80g	54	16g
sweets (candies)			
jelly beans	small bag	80	29g
Skittles	small bag	70	27g
taco shells	2	68	16g
taro, raw	80g	54	16g
tuna	120g	0	0g
water biscuits	2 bisc	63	12g
watermelon	150g	72	8g
yam, boiled	80g	51	24g
yogurt, fruit	200g	33	26g

index